HENRY PURCELL

Henry Purcell. A drawing attributed to Kneller. (*Reproduced by courtesy of the Trustees of the British Museum.*)

HENRY PURCELL

1659-1695

Essays on his Music

edited by
IMOGEN HOLST

LONDON
OXFORD UNIVERSITY PRESS
New York Toronto
1959

Oxford University Press, Amen House, London E.C.4

GLASGOW NEW YORK TORONTO MELBOURNE WELLINGTON
BOMBAY CALCUTTA MADRAS KARACHI KUALA LUMPUR
CAPE TOWN IBADAN NAIROBI ACCRA

Printed in Great Britain

PREFACE

This collection of essays was planned as a result of trying to solve some of the practical problems of editing Purcell's works for performance. Even those of us who have been brought up on his music are still woefully ignorant when it comes to such questions as whether a note should be doubly-dotted or whether it should be a flat or a natural. One longs to know what balance of singers and players Purcell had at his first performances and whether certain parts were sung by a counter-tenor or by an ordinary tenor with light, easy top notes. Perhaps our greatest need, when puzzled by the conflicting guesses of different editors of his music, is to know where to find the manuscripts, and, having found them, to know how to recognize if they are autographs or not.

The following essays answer a great many questions, and I am very grateful to the singers, players, composers, and writers who have found time to contribute, from their practical experience, to this tercentenary volume.

Many others have helped in the writing of this book. I am particularly grateful to the Tokyo representatives of the British Council for their kindness in making enquiries about the Nanki library, to Mr. Anthony Gishford for his encouragement in the early stages of this book, and to the Oxford University Press for their patience in the later stages. I also wish to thank Messrs. Faber & Faber Ltd. for permission to quote from *Poetry and Drama*, by T. S. Eliot, and Messrs. Routledge & Kegan Paul Ltd. for permission to quote from *Problems of Art*, by Suzanne Langer.

I. H.

Aldeburgh, September, 1958

CONTENTS

LIST OF ILLUSTRATIONS

I

Homage to the British Orpheus

PETER PEARS

The ingredients in the magic brew of song are words and notes. A gift of melody is often enough to give great pleasure; the correct accentuation of words can inform and suggest; the revelation of sense through sound and of sound in sense is given to few to achieve. None would deny Purcell's melodic genius; there is plentiful witness to it throughout his work for the stage, both instrumental and vocal. 'I attempt from love's sickness to fly', 'If music be the food of love', 'They tell us that yon mighty powers', 'If love's a sweet passion' are only the beginning of a long list of jewels. Purcell was content often, as Dowland was before him, to use a simple dance-form as a song, and also to turn a dance into a song or a song into a dance, e.g. the Hornpipe from the Fairy Queen which was used for 'There's not a swain'.[1] The four bar phrases of 'If love's a sweet passion' link it to the dance; no one has written a more singable melody to fit into twenty-four bars.

The dance-forms at Purcell's disposal were less favourable for the settings of songs of character than the Pavans and Galliards which Dowland used. The heavy down beats of the Pavan easily suggest melancholy moods, and Dowland

[1] An American musician, Mr. Jonathan Edmunds, has fitted contemporary words to some of Purcell's Ayres for the Theatre and Incidental dances. Some of them go very well, more particularly the straighter dance-forms.

was not a man to miss a chance so much to his fancy. Purcell's dances were more extrovert and better suited to gay songs and sweet sentiments.

When Purcell wishes to elaborate slightly a simple dance-form for the setting of words, his felicity can be quite extraordinary. Consider such a popular favourite as 'I attempt from love's sickness to fly'. Only a consummate genius could unite such cunning with such delicious freshness. First, the little dove-like flight of notes on the word 'fly' (a straight run and a twist to escape) colours the vocal line; next, the very lack of symmetry in the rhythm (five bars plus seven bars in the refrain, five plus six and four plus six in the verses) gives a wayward movement to the song, while the fall at the end of each line adds a touch of hopeless weakness to remind the listener of the vain attempt at escape from love's sickness. As often happens in Purcell's music, the major key sounds sad; compare his use of minor keys for joy. Many of Purcell's shorter songs are in dance form slightly elaborated at cadences, prolonged by repetitions of key words. These are often surprisingly difficult to perform because the phrases need very clever shaping, and can easily sound strange and dull. 'I take no pleasure', 'Olinda', 'See how the fading glories' are songs of this type. The relationship between words and music has to be very carefully examined, and the poise has to be found and held in those tricky wayward phrases which are continually going out of the straight.

To find an example of Purcell's direct magic with words and music, one need go no further than *Dido and Aeneas*.

> Fear no danger to ensue,
> The Hero loves as well as you,

sings Belinda in lines of no very special distinction. But

Nahum Tate knew what he was about, and he gave Purcell verses of a neutral, passive quality which were fair game for a real composer. In the hands of a lesser man, the result might well have been deadly: Purcell uses the words for his musical ends and with false verbal accents gives a brilliant lilt to the passage and offers us a melody of striking and memorable quality. (This air is surely the father of Handel's setting of Milton's 'Come and trip it as you go on the light fantastic toe' in *L'Allegro*.) Other composers of the period use all the stock devices also, as Purcell did; but he almost always transforms them by the magic of genius into sensitive living creations. His vocal line is more inventive within its chosen shape; compare, for instance, Blow's *Self-Banished* with Purcell's 'How blest are shepherds'. His figured bass seldom fails to give an inventive player legitimately lively ideas for realization. It is hardly necessary to remark that a great danger of the figured-bass style lies in the responsibility that is thrown on the keyboard player. If he is dull and inept, even the best music can sound very tedious. In particular, the movements over a ground bass can die from lack of invention. The splendid *Divine Hymns*, too, need a feeling for colour from the keyboard to match the wonderfully expressive vocal line. We have the Air 'Here the deities approve' over a ground, transcribed for the solo harpsichord by the composer, to show us how ravishingly Purcell would have accompanied such a piece himself.

It would seem that at no time was he not a master of dramatic character-painting in recitative. From the earliest anthems to the last song that he set, Purcell seems to have had a flair for the creation of character in music quite without equal (one is tempted to say) at any time. But alas! he had all too little opportunity for exercising this prodigious talent. *Dido and Aeneas*, some of the religious pieces, some of the incidental music,—this is all that can be included in the dramatic category. Most of the stage music, nearly all of *King Arthur*, *Dioclesian*, *The Tempest*, *The Fairy Queen* is masque music, delightful and skilful and inventive and adorable, but lacking the sustained intensity that fills the music of character and situation. Nor was this anything but right; dramatic music of the intensity of *Dido* or 'Job's Curse' would have been quite out of place in *King Arthur* or *The Fairy Queen*. One can see from songs like 'The Fatal Hour', 'Sweeter than Roses' and 'From rosy bowers' what Purcell could have done with the operatic situations involving the most pointed characterizations; one can also imagine what effect his lyrical and expressive airs over a ground would have had in their proper perspective in a Gluck-ish or Mozartian opera libretto. No opera seria of Gluck has a more intense and un-artificial air than Dido's Lament or 'O Solitude', composed though these are in the 'ancient and learned' form of a Ground. The seventeenth century was in its musical forms much freer than the eighteenth century; it was a period which musicologists like to label in a derogatory tone 'transitional', nearly always sensitive and lively, in which a genius such as Purcell could find all he wanted for the exercise of his talents, even in opera, until the social conventions of a capital in which a man of letters (Dryden) was incomparably more important than a musician put Purcell into a secondary position in the theatre. Lamentations are no doubt vain, one should not bewail the crackling fustian of Dryden's *King Arthur*; might one not rather suggest that Mr. W. H. Auden, the Dryden of our time, should leave tampering with Mozart's untouchable *Flute* and consider refashioning the stage framework for Purcell's lovely music?

When the background to Purcell's dramatic songs is

implicit in the text (e.g. 'Mad Bess', 'From rosy bowers')
he is at his superb best. Some of the poems which he set
dramatically have so little character that even Purcell can
hardly reveal the personality of the singer. In the *Divine
Hymns*, however, with the whole Bible as his stage and some
thundering texts by contemporary bishops comparable
with, though superior to, Bach's cantata texts, Purcell
created dramatic scenes of great vividness. 'Job's Curse',
'Saul at Endor', and 'The Blessed Virgin's Expostulation'
are full of examples of astonishing invention. The Prologue
and Epilogue to 'Saul' bring the characters on to the stage
and take them off again in music of perfectly-timed myster-
iousness. Samuel's appearance is calculated to present the
new dark colour of the bass voice to the most impressive
effect imaginable. Saul's high distress and the witch's wails
are dramatic strokes of a master-composer for the stage. The
Virgin's ariettas are concise and beautifully contrasted, and
her reiterated cries of 'Gabriel' are amazing each time one
hears them.

What makes, for instance, 'Job's Curse' so impressive a
work? In the long recitative, the declamation is of the most
vivid kind, where each word has its proper dramatic
accent (as against the natural accent) and yet fits into an
impressive musical pattern.

> Let the night perish, cursed be the morn
> Wherein 'twas said, There is a man-child born!

Slowly the melodic line emerges and climbs over towards
the hammer-strokes of those last words, and then we are off
to an agony of prophetic denunciations in a music of wild
tortuousness. The voice moves through intervals strange and
unexpected; the harmony continually changes; it is difficult
to imagine that the eighteenth century is only a decade

away. After the long recitative with its many picturesque points and the wonderful section starting

> Why did I not when first my mother's womb
> Discard'd me drop down into my tomb?

Purcell gives us a beautiful resigned air full of Job's longing for the peace of the grave, an air where each word is so placed that its whole meaning seems to penetrate each individual note. An extraordinary intensity emerges which comes from the complete wedding of the sound and sense of the words with a melody of great musical beauty. It is, to use Dryden's phrase, 'Musick, the exaltation of Poetry'.

This magic gift of Purcell's with words and music cannot be explained any more than Schubert's can. It is easy enough to say that he found in words the sound-picture (line, colour, and proportion) which was translatable into song. How he found this, and his method of translating, are his secrets and his copyright. There is really no need to probe; it is enough to love, in this his tercentenary year, our incomparable Orpheus Britannicus.

2

On Realizing the Continuo in Purcell's Songs

BENJAMIN BRITTEN

In practically every one of our concerts, given the length
of three continents over the last twenty years, Peter Pears
and I have included a group of Purcell's songs. Although
they were not included for chauvinistic reasons, it has been
nice to find that foreign audiences accept these English
songs alongside those of their own great classic song-writers.
It is pleasant to get cheers at the end of Purcell's 'Alleluia'
in the home of Schubert and Wolf, requests for a repeat of
'Man is for the woman made' in the birthplace of Mozart,
appreciative giggles at the end of 'There's not a swain of
the Plain' in Fauré's home town, and an impressive silence
as the last bars of 'Job's Curse' die away in Düsseldorf,
where Schumann spent many years. And not only in foreign
places; in England too—where, to our shame, the music
of Purcell is still shockingly unknown. It is unknown
because so much of it is unobtainable in print, and so much of
what is available is in realizations which are frankly dull and
out of date. Because all Purcell's solo songs, secular and
sacred, as well as his many big scenas, have to be realized.
We have these wonderful vocal parts, and fine strong basses,
but nothing in between (even the figures for the harmony
are often missing). If the tradition of improvisation from a
figured bass were not lost, this would not be so serious, but

to most people now, until a worked-out edition is available, these cold, unfilled-in lines mean nothing, and the incredible beauty and vitality, and infinite variety of these hundreds of songs go undiscovered. Therefore over these many years I have myself realized about twenty secular songs (mostly from *Orpheus Britannicus*), a few sacred songs, four of the big *Divine Hymns* (from the *Harmonia Sacra*) and half-a-dozen duets (some taken from the dramatic works reprinted separately by Purcell's widow in *Orpheus Britannicus*)—all with piano. I have also realized for other occasions the *Golden Sonata*, and continuo parts of the fine *Welcome Song* of 1687, and Purcell's masterpiece, *Dido and Aeneas*, for harpsichord. There is also a sequence of songs, a Suite from *Orpheus Britannicus*, where I realized the figured bass for strings.

Never have I attempted the ultimate realization of any of these songs. Since the accompaniments were originally intended to be improvised, they must be personal and immediate—and as we know only too well how ephemeral fashions are, how quickly tastes change, so each generation must want its own realizations. (I have myself in several cases changed my mind about my own efforts and after a few years rewritten them.) The most I have hoped for is to have drawn attention to some of these wonderful and useful songs by a lively enough version, and hope therefore that eventually other people will like these songs enough to arrange them themselves.

I have no theories as to how this should be done. But in the light of my experience here are a few deductions. It is an important rule of the game that one should stick to the actual notes of the bass (with allowable changing of the length of the notes—it seems in those days they were not too particular about this—and changing of the octave, such as could be done by different registrations on the harpsichord.) And one must of course complete the harmonies in the way the figures indicate. If there are gaps in these (and there are many) a knowledge of the period and the composer's personal style should help. But just a filling in by these harmonies above the correct notes is not enough; one dimension is still lacking, the dimension of one's personal reaction to the song, which in former days would have been supplied by improvisation. This dimension comes from the *texture* of the accompaniment, the *way* the harmonies are filled in. If one is realizing for a piano it is important to be aware of the difference of sound from harpsichord and string bass, for which most of the songs would have been written. There must be compensation for the lack of sustaining power of the actual bass notes (repeated notes, octaves, trills, tremolandi for crescendi &c.), as well as an awareness of the difference between the plucked and hammered strings. Actually the sound that Purcell expected, this harpsichord sound, can give one ideas—dry clear arpeggios, grace-notes, octave doublings, sudden contrasts in dynamics or range, and that wonderful short staccato. However, the principal factors determining the texture are the form of the songs, the shapes of phrases in the voice part or the bass, and of course the mood of the words.

If the songs are simple verse songs, or songs not broken up into many sections, the accompaniment should reflect this by keeping to a consistent style. In 'I attempt from love's sickness to fly' I have supported the beautiful melody with simple continuous four-part harmony (with occasional doublings), with the top line occasionally moving in quavers suggested by the tune and the mood of the song. In 'Fairest Isle' I have used Purcell's own harmonies taken from his choral version (in *King Arthur*), with new keyboard spacing. In each successive verse of 'Man is for the woman made' I have invented new figuration to match the increasing dottiness of the words. In 'How blest are shepherds' and 'On the brow of Richmond Hill' the repetitions (I suggest, echoes) of each section of the tune have newly spaced harmonies to support it. The solo version of 'Turn then thine eyes' has rapid quaver triplets to introduce the coloratura of the voice part. The lively ♪ ♩ of 'will on thy cheek appear' is echoed on the piano. The elegant coquetry of 'Pious Celinda' suggested to me an ironic eighteenth-century phrase with a turn and grace note, which interrupts the amusing vocal line. 'Hark the echoing air' suggested imitations of trumpets and oboes (as did the 'Sound the Trumpet' duet) and the 'clapping of wings' suggested quick, snappy grace notes. In the songs with ostinato basses, which are many, I try to establish the ostinato clearly to begin with, and then colour each new image with new figuration—the 'snakes drop' in staccato thirds in 'Music for a while' after a clear four-octave start; in the 'Evening Hymn' the harmonies change very slowly and figuration is only gradually introduced.

In the form which Purcell perfected—the continuous movement made up of independent, short sections mysteriously linked by subtle contrasts of key, mood, and rhythm— the accompaniment must follow and emphasize these contrasts. Each miniature section of 'Sweeter than Roses' has its own figuration; the cool arpeggios of the 'roses'— in the short interlude, echoing the singer's first melting phrase—the growing intensity of 'warm' and the firm cadential 'kiss'; the 'trembling' is in oscillating sixths; high shivering chords 'freeze'; 'fire' has lively crackling chords; trumpets accompany the 'victorious love', and dizzy whirling quavers 'all, all, all is love'. This perhaps sounds naïve, but Purcell has himself suggested some such musical pictures in the voice and bass parts, and besides he has provided in these given parts a firm and secure musical structure which can safely hold together and make sense of one's wildest fantasies. This is only one of many similar cases. Perhaps the most beautiful and certainly one of the wildest, is 'Mad Bess'. Here to start, to finish, and to introduce many of the sections, I have used a scurrying semiquaver passage based on the first vocal phrase. Dramatically it can be said to suggest the movements of poor demented Bess.

In the *Divine Hymns* I have used the same kind of technique, but with a less exaggerated fantasy, since the moods are mostly less extreme. 'Lord, what is man' is in three fully worked out sections. The austere recitative which starts this fine Hymn I have accompanied quite barely: a turn for each of the long pedal notes—later a trill at the more animated 'Reveal ye glorious spirits'—chords at each change of harmony; and I echo the vocal run as 'joy' fades out into 'astonishment'. In the arioso 'Oh, for a quill' the little quaver passages in the piano part are all suggested by the voice or bass part, and by the intense though subdued mood of longing. The final 'Hallelujah' starts quietly—in figuration, largely octave doubling of the bass. I have added semiquaver figures as the momentum grows, and as the movement fades out into a soft ecstatic finish (which is the way we always do it) the right hand crosses and re-crosses the voice in flowing semiquavers.

The splendid opening tune of 'We sing to Him' suggests to me the singing of a thousand voices, so the accompaniment is in full ringing chords.

In 'Job's Curse' I have taken the liberty of repeating the last four bass bars as a little codetta after the voice has finished, in order to let the impact of this tremendous scena die away more gradually. It is however printed in small notes and can be omitted very easily. Similarly in 'I attempt from love's sickness to fly', that perfect opening song for a recital, I have preluded the song by a few bars; practical experience has shown us that this is necessary in order to accustom the audience to the style of the music, the sweet, subtle mood before the voice starts. The two little ariosi in 'The Blessed Virgin's Expostulation' are more contrapuntal—at 'me Judah's daughter', canonical, with the left hand gently filling in the harmonies.

One of Purcell's most elaborate dramatic Scenas is 'Saul and the Witch at Endor'. Misty slow-moving quavers at the start bind together the three voices, united in setting the gloomy scene. When they separate into their three individual characters I have used the simple device of different registers to add to the characterizations—the ghost of Samuel almost disappearing off the bottom of the piano.

'Celemene', the Dialogue for soprano and tenor from *Oroonoko* ('sung by the boy and the girl') could not be a greater contrast. The children prattle away about the puzzles of love, and I have followed the onomatopoeia of the voice parts: the heart-beats, the trembling, the touching. A five-finger exercise matches the innocence of 'When you wash yourself and play . . .' Again in 'I spy Celia' I have tried to follow every instruction in this young person's guide to love.

In the Suite from *Orpheus Britannicus* in which I arranged the figured basses for strings the problem was really the same as if realizing for piano, but with the big difference of thinking in terms of strings. At the start of 'Let sullen Discord smile' I added a viola part to the other strings because of the absence of a keyboard instrument. In the original the upper strings were dropped at the entry of the voice. I continue them in simple four-part harmony, adding *martello* scale passages at 'let war devote this day to peace'. In 'Why should men quarrel' strings *pizzicato* fill out the harmony in between the spiky flute figuration and the cello solo. 'So when the glittering queen of Night' has the harmony filled out in the divided muted cellos and double bass. Against this funeral march-like background the voice and three solo strings stand out clearly like stars on a dark night. The introduction of 'Thou tun'st this world' is originally for two oboes and continuo. I have given the bass line to a bassoon and not completed the harmony. When the voice enters, the strings take over with simple detached chords, only occasionally flowing into figuration. At the end of this typically Purcellian song in a gay minor key, we repeat the second half of the introduction (as before on wind instruments alone). The splendid 'Sound Fame' has a rousing, but not Handelian, trumpet solo against one of Purcell's barest ostinatos. The latter I have given to a second string orchestra in octaves (at the end in four octaves). The first orchestra plays counterpoints and occasionally pizzicato block harmonies; finally joining the trumpet in diatonic semiquavers.

I know there are many other ways of realizing Purcell's figured basses—a highly distinguished series is now being brought out by my friends Michael Tippett and Walter Bergmann. I hope there will be many more, and done with plenty of boldness of imagination, for what has kept so many of these wonderful treasures locked up in obscurity has been creative dullness or too much reverence. Purcell would have hated these two qualities above all; at least, that is the feeling one has after getting to know him through even these few works.

3

New Light on 'Dido and Aeneas'

ERIC WALTER WHITE

To those who believe that *Dido and Aeneas* is a masterpiece of English opera, authoritative information about its music and libretto is of considerable importance.

No score was published in Purcell's lifetime—in fact, the first published version was an incomplete one printed by the Musical Antiquarian Society in 1841—and today the main authority for the music resides in certain copyists' manuscripts. Writing in the preface to the Purcell Society edition of *Dido and Aeneas*, 1889, Dr. W. H. Cummings claimed to have in his possession 'a MS. score of the opera written probably in Purcell's time'. After his death, this score was sold at Sotheby's in 1917 under the following description:

Purcell (H) Dido and Aeneas, MS., with musical notes, half calf, uncut, SÆC. XVIII

It was acquired by the Marquis Tokugawa and shipped to Japan in 1920, where for some years it remained in the Nanki Music Library. It is not clear where it is now,[1] so Cummings's claim cannot be checked.

This is unfortunate, because Cummings appears to have been an unreliable guide to the other important manuscript score—the one that formerly belonged to the Rev. Sir Frederick Ouseley and is now in the Library of St. Michael's College, Tenbury Wells. He refers to this manuscript also

[1] News of this MS. is given in Appendix C. [Editor.]

in the preface to the Purcell Society edition of *Dido and Aeneas* and calls it 'a fine MS. score written by John Travers, about 1720.' In fact, the name of John Travers is mentioned nowhere in this manuscript; and the anonymous scribe's handwriting differs in a number of marked particulars from Travers's own authenticated hand. Handwriting tests are notoriously difficult to apply with complete success; but in this case the apparently gratuitous attribution to Travers is probably also faulted by the paper on which the manuscript is written. This being watermarked 'J. WHATMAN' must date from the latter part of the eighteenth century.

But the fact that Cummings was wrong about the attribution of the Tenbury MS. and that it belongs to a later date than hitherto suspected do not necessarily detract from its value. Whoever the scribe may have been, his copy was a 'fair' one in the best sense of that word. Not only is it clean and clear, but internal evidence shows it was based on a very early score—possibly Purcell's own original manuscript as adapted for use in the theatre. The style of notation and the restricted use of figuration imply that the original must date from the end of the seventeenth or beginning of the eighteenth century. The plentiful stage directions certainly refer to an actual stage production.

When Nahum Tate came to write the libretto, he was already familiar with the story of Dido and Aeneas, since some years previously he had based the action of his first play on the fourth book of the Aeneid, but on the advice of certain friends (as he explains in the preface) he had altered the names of the characters and the scene of the action, the tragedy in its transformed guise appearing as *Brutus of Alba* (1678). His libretto for Purcell's opera, which made use of some of the material that had appeared in the earlier play, was originally brought out as an eight-page folio pamphlet (perhaps for private circulation as no publisher's name is given) with the following inscription at the head of p. 1 of the text:

AN OPERA

Perform'd at

MR. JOSIAS PRIEST's Boarding-School at
CHELSEY

By Young Gentlewomen.

The Words Made by Mr. NAT. TATE.

The Musick Composed by Mr. Henry Purcell.

Only a single copy of this publication is known, and that is now in the Library of the Royal College of Music. As the opera was probably performed for the first time in 1689 or 1690, it is reasonable to suppose that this libretto, though undated, was published at the same time. This dating is borne out by the fact that the Epilogue that Thomas D'Urfey specially wrote for this school production and which has the following specific reference to the Revolution of 1688-89:

> *Rome* may allow strange Tricks to please her Sons,
> But we are Protestants and *English* Nuns——

was included in a collection entitled *New Poems* published in 1690. The opera had to wait over ten years for its first professional performance, which was given in 1700 at the Theatre in Lincoln's Inn Fields by Thomas Betterton's company in the course of a production of Shakespeare's *Measure for Measure*. By then Purcell had been dead for over four years. The opera libretto was included in the quarto edition of the play published the same year; and this version differs from the earlier text in certain material ways.

At this point a word should be said about the title of the opera. As has been pointed out above, the original libretto is untitled, though it is possible that the text of the libretto may have been preceded by a title-page now lost. *Dido and Aeneas* is definitely mentioned as the title of the opera in D'Urfey's published Epilogue. In the *Measure for Measure* quarto the title is *The Loves of Dido and Aeneas*, and the work is subtitled a masque. When it was revived in 1704 for at least two performances that were independent of *Measure for Measure*, the advertisements referred to it as the Masque of Aeneas and Dido. The fact that the title given to the opera in the Tenbury MS. is *The Loves of Aeneas and Dido* may mean that the score from which this MS. was copied was the one specially prepared for these 1704 performances at Lincoln's Inn Fields.

Although the 1700 text of the libretto has been public property for over two and a half centuries, no one interested in English opera generally and *Dido and Aeneas* in particular seems to have paid any special attention to it. Either its existence has been ignored; or where it has been known, comment has been inaccurate and misleading. For instance, Cummings in his preface to the Purcell Society edition of the score mentioned the fact that some of the pieces in the opera had at times been 'divorced from the work and introduced into stage plays, without regard to their appropriateness; for example, "Fear no danger" was thrust into Shakespeare's *Measure for Measure*, as may be seen from a copy of the music of the duet published in 1700'. This is a misunderstanding. The number in question was published by Walsh as an extract from the opera as played in this special production of *Measure for Measure*. Alfred Loewenberg in his *Annals of Opera* (1943) stated that *Dido and Aeneas* 'was given as an interlude in C. Gildon's version of *Measure for Measure*'. This is inaccurate in so far as it implies that the opera was given between acts of the play. As will be seen, Gildon did his best to integrate it into the action. Harold Child was nearer the truth when in his note on the stage history of the play (written for the Cambridge New Shakespeare in 1922) he said that Gildon's adaptation 'was so successful as to be given eight times, largely owing, perhaps, to the four "entertainments of musick" (three of them taken from Purcell's *Dido and Aeneas*) with which it was diversified'. But even here Child was at fault in that he failed to realize that the fourth entertainment was an integral part of Tate's libretto for *Dido and Aeneas*, though whether or not it was set by Purcell is a moot point. Edward J. Dent (in *Foundations of English Opera*, 1928) realized that *Dido and Aeneas* was 'inserted as a masque into Gildon's adaptation of *Measure for Measure*', but implied that it was given only once in that form, whereas in fact it was not only performed several times during the 1700 season, but was revived on its own at the Theatre in Lincoln's Inn Fields in 1704 and may have been played at the newly built Queen's Theatre in the Haymarket when *Measure for Measure* was revived there in 1706.[1]

During the last quarter of the seventeenth century, the theatre in Dorset Garden, which Sir Christopher Wren had built for the Duke's Men in 1673, served as the chief centre of operatic production in London; and it was there that Purcell's dramatic operas, *The Prophetess*, *King Arthur*, and *The Fairy Queen*, were produced in the early 1690s. By 1695, the year of Purcell's death, however, the fortunes of the Theatre had started to wane; and in that year too

---

[1] This latter performance is rather doubtful, however, since the advertisement specifies '*Measure for Measure* written by the famous Beaumont and Fletcher with the Masque of Acis and Galatea', &c., and this may mean that *Acis and Galatea* took the place of *The Loves of Dido and Aeneas*, though there would be nothing unusual in adding an extra masque as an afterpiece.

Betterton, who had been acting with the United Companies at the Theatre Royal, Drury Lane, since 1682, moved to Lincoln's Inn Fields with a number of experienced players, leaving a comparatively young and immature company behind at Drury Lane. He erected a theatre by subscription within the walls of Lisle's Tennis Court, and opened with a new play by William Congreve, *Love for Love*. The competition between the two companies was keen. One of the first things the Drury Lane players did was to transfer some of Purcell's semi-operas from Dorset Garden, adding *The Prophetess* to their repertory in 1697 and *King Arthur* in 1698. (There is no record of a revival of *The Fairy Queen* at Drury Lane until 1703, when only a single act was performed, presumably because the score seems to have been mislaid shortly after Purcell's death.) Lincoln's Inn Fields retaliated by mounting opera too. The rivalry between the two houses is referred to in a Dialogue called *A Comparison between the Two Stages* (1702), which has sometimes been (erroneously) attributed to Gildon:

Sullen. . . . The *Opera* now possesses the Stage [i.e. at Drury Lane] and after a hard Struggle, at length it prevail'd, and something more than Charges came in every Night: The Quality, who are always Lovers of good Musick, flock hither, and by almost a total revolt from the other *House*, give this new Life, and set it in some eminency above the *New*; this was a sad mortification to the old Stagers in *Lincolns-Inn-Fields*, but at length they too—

Critic. Nay, there I will prevent you good Mr. *Sullen*; I must have the Honour of this Speech. At last, (as you say) the old Stagers moulded a piece of Pastry work of their own, and made a kind of Lenten Feast with their *Rinaldo & Armida*; this surpriz'd not only *Drury-Lane*, but indeed all the Town, no body ever dreaming of an *Opera* there.

The piece of pastry-work referred to was *Rinaldo and Armida* (with music by John Eccles to a libretto by John Dennis, 1698); and this was followed two years later by *The Loves of Dido and Aeneas.*

The rivalry between the two houses expressed itself also in choice of plays. Betterton was particularly successful in Shakespeare: Drury Lane retaliated with Ben Jonson. To quote once more from *A Comparison between the Two Stages*:

Sullen. Well, this lucky hit of *Batterton's* put *D. Lane* to a nonplus: *Shakespear's* Ghost was rais'd at the New-house, and he seem'd to inhabit it for ever: What's to be done then? . . . Then they fell to task on the *Fox*, the *Alchymist*, and *Silent Woman*, who had lain twenty years in Peace, they drew up these in Battalia against *Harry* the 4th and *Harry* the 8th, and then the Fight began. Now do you proceed—

Critic. The Battel continued a long time doubtful, and Victory hovering over both Camps, *Batterton* Sollicits for some Auxiliaries from the same Author, and then he flanks his Enemy with *Measure* for *Measure*.

Measure for Measure, or, *Beauty the Best Advocate*, a 'very much alter'd' version of Shakespeare's play 'with additions of several Entertainments of Musick' was acted by Betterton's company at the Lincoln's Inn Fields Theatre early in 1700. The plot was altered, the scene changed from Vienna to Turin, and the comic characters and low-life scenes omitted, their place being taken by the musical entertainments. Although the adaptor's name was not given on the title-page of the quarto that was published that summer, he is known to have been Charles Gildon from an advertisement appended to Gildon's *Love's Victim* (1701) which ran as follows:

Measure for Measure a Comedy alter'd from *Beaumont & Fletcher* by **Mr.** *Gildon.*

Subsequent Shakespearian adaptations at Lincoln's Inn Fields included *The Merchant of Venice*, altered by George Granville, Lord Lansdowne, and retitled *The Jew of Venice* (1701), which contained a masque of Peleus and Thetis, and a dull and vulgar version of *Twelfth Night* by William Burnaby called *Love Betray'd* (1703). This too was intended to include a masque, though it appears to have been omitted in actual performance.

The Loves of Dido and Aeneas was inserted into the action of *Measure for Measure* as if it were a masque, or succession of masques. The whole of Tate's libretto—that is the three-act opera together with the classical-pastoral prologue—was worked into the text of Gildon's adaptation in the form of four separate entertainments, the first, second and third entertainments (roughly equivalent to Acts I, II, and III of the opera) being introduced as a series of diversions played before Angelo in Act I, Scene 1, Act II, Scene 2, and Act III, Scene 1, respectively, and the fourth entertainment (viz. the classical-pastoral prologue of the libretto) coming after Act V at the end of the play. Although the first three entertainments are placed near the end of their particular scenes, the action is resumed, however briefly, at the end of each entertainment. 'Begin the *Opera*, the Deputy attends', says Lucio; and that is the cue for the first entertainment, at the end of which Angelo says, 'This Musick is no Cure for my Distemper' &c.— 'Come let 'em begin', cries Angelo at the beginning of the second entertainment; and when it is over, he pursues a striking analogy between Dido and Isabella:

> All will not do: All won't devert my Pain,
> The Wound enlarges by these Medicines,
> 'Tis She alone can yield the Healing Balm.
> This Scene just hits my case; her Brothers danger,
> Is here the storm must furnish Blest occasion;

> But when, my Dido, I've possess'd thy Charms,
> I then will throw thee from my glutted Arms,
> And think no more on all thy soothing Harms.

At the beginning of the third entertainment Angelo again commands 'Let them begin' and then comments 'No *Isabella* yet?' A stage direction follows: '*They all sit, and the Third Musick. Before 'tis quite done*, Isabella *enters*.' The final chorus 'With drooping wings' is followed immediately by Angelo's comment,

> 'I see my Ev'ning Star of Love appear.
> This is no place to try my last Effort', &c.

Even the fourth entertainment, which comes right at the end of the play, is followed by a brief eight-line speech of the Duke's.

This technique recalls the way Elkanah Settle and Matthew Locke introduced the masque of Orpheus and Euridice into *The Empress of Morocco* (1673) at the climax of the action; but whereas Orpheus and Euridice was a complete operatic scene in itself and was played without a break, there can be no doubt that in the case of Gildon's adaptation the dramatic scheme of *Dido and Aeneas* was adversely affected by the necessity of separating the acts with substantial chunks of Shakespeare's play. So it is not surprising that shortly afterwards *The Loves of Dido and Aeneas* was divorced from *Measure for Measure* and presented on its own at Lincoln's Inn Fields as a masque following *The Anatomist* on 29 January 1704 and *The Man of Mode* on 8 April the same year.

Nor were the exposition and unfolding of the action of the opera helped by a transposition of two scenes, for which Gildon was presumably responsible. In Tate's original libretto the action runs as follows:

But in Gildon's adaptation, Scenes 1 and 2 of Act II are transposed, the two scenes in their reversed order forming the whole of the second entertainment. This transposition is such an error from the dramatic point of view that one naturally wonders why he should have countenanced it.

One possible explanation is that there are certain stage effects in the Cave scene that may have made it preferable for that scene to follow the Grove scene in the Lincoln's Inn Fields production. In the 1700 quarto, the Cave scene opens with the stage direction, '*The Cave rises. The Witches appear*'. After the Echo Dance of Furies, there is the direction, '*At the end of the Dance Six Furies sinks. The four open the Cave fly up*'.[1] Specific directions regarding rising, sinking and flying are not to be found at this point in the 1689 libretto, presumably because only a limited range of stage effects was possible in Mr. Priest's School. But it is clear from the stage directions in *Rinaldo and Armida*, which was played in the Lincoln's Inn Fields Theatre towards the end of 1698, that after its recent adaptation the stage there was fully equipped for rising, sinking, and flying effects. In fact, incidental music was sometimes played under the stage, as appears from a direction '*The Serpent and Bases softly under*

[1] This stage direction gives a fascinating glimpse of the choreographer's intentions for the Echo Dance. The misprint 'open', most probably meant for 'over', suggests that there may have been four dancers above the roof of the cave, imitating—a bar later—the movements of the six dancers on the floor of the stage; their gestures, clearly defined against the sky, conveying a visual 'echo'. [Editor.]

the Stage', and this device could also have been used in *The Loves of Dido and Aeneas* for the Echo Dance of the Furies. In any case, it may have been more convenient from the standpoint of stage management at Lincoln's Inn Fields for the Cave scene to follow the Grove scene, so that the sinking and flying and rising and echo effects could come at the end of this particular entertainment rather than in the middle.

This contention seems to be supported by the Tenbury MS., where the layout of the action (the Prologue being absent) is as follows:

Act I, Scene 1—The Palace
Scene 2—The Cave
Act II, Scene 1—The Grove
Act III, Scene 1—The Ships

It looks as if the Cave scene had been restored to its rightful place in the original score, while the stage directions for flying and sinking remained—in the Tenbury MS. the direction after the Echo Dance of Furies is '*Thunder and Lightning horrid Musick*.[1] *The Furies sink down in the Cave the Rest fly up*'—so it still seemed convenient to make the end of the Cave scene the place for an act division, or (as the Tenbury MS. specifies) 'The End of the first part'. This is probably the way the opera was given at the two 1704 performances at Lincoln's Inn Fields mentioned above.

Various persons have drawn attention to the apparently unset chorus and dance at the end of Act II. In Tate's 1689 libretto the passage runs as follows:

> *The Sorceress and her Inchanteress.*
> *Cho.* Then since our Charmes have Sped,
>   A Merry Dance be led

---

[1] *Rinaldo and Armida* also has the stage direction, '*Thunder and Lightning, and Horrid Musick alternately*'.

Dido. The Skies are Clouded, heark, how Thunder   [Thunder.
    Rends the Mountain Oaks assunder;
    Haft, haft to Town, this open Field,
    No shelter from the Storm can yield.   [Exit.

The Spirit *of the Sorceress descends to* Æneas *in likeness of* Mercury.

Spir. Stay Prince and hear great Joves Command.
    He Summons thee this Night away.
Æn. To Night?
Spir. To Night thou must forsake this Land,
    The Angry God will brook no longer stay.
    Jove Commands thee, waft no more
    In Loves delights those Precious Hours,
    Allow'd by the Almighty Powers,
    To gain the Hesperian shore,
    And Ruin'd Troy restore.
Æn. Jove's Commands shall be Obey'd,
    To Night our Anchors shall be weigh'd;
    But ha! What Language can I try,
    My injur'd Queen to pacify?
    No sooner she resignes her Heart,
    But from her Arms I'm forc't to part.
    How can so hard a Fate be took,
    One Night Enjoy'd, the next forsook?
    Yours be the Blame, ye Gods, for I,
    Obey your will —— but with more ease cou'd dye.
    " Direct me, friends, what Choice to make,
    " Since Love and Fame together press me,
    " And with equal Force distress me.
    " Say what Party I shall take.
1 Fr. Resistless Jove Commands ——
2 Fr. But Love
    More Resistless then Jove's.
Æn. But Fame Alcander.
2 Fr. Fame's a Bubble,
    Honour but a Glorious Trouble,
    A vain Pride of Destroying,
    Alarming and Arming,
    And Toiling and Moiling,
    And never Enjoying.
1 Fr. 'Twas that gave Hector,
2 Fr. What?
1 Fr. Renown and Fame.
2 Fr. An empty Name,
    And Lamentable Fate.

                         1 Fr. 'Twas

I. A page from Gildon's adaptation of *Measure for Measure* (1700), showing part of the additional scene in *Dido and Aeneas*. (*Reproduced by courtesy of the Trustees of the British Museum.*)

By the Nymphs of *Carthage* to please us.
They shall all Dance to ease us.
A Dance that shall make the Spheres to wonder,
Rending these fair Groves asunder.
  The Groves Dance.

Dent (in *Foundations of English Opera*) gave it as his opinion that 'the inconclusive tonality' of Aeneas's preceding recitative, with which the act at present ends, 'suggests that Purcell may have originally intended to set the chorus, but perhaps cut it out, feeling that the despair of Aeneas made a more dramatic end to the act'. Dent did not see anything unstylistic in this extraordinarily non-classical procedure, though he regretted Purcell did not 'contrive his recitative so as to end the act in the key in which it began'.

Benjamin Britten went further than Dent. After he had made a special realization of the score for the English Opera Group revival of the opera during the Festival of Britain, 1951, he issued a statement (dated 4 April 1951) in which he said:

Anyone who has taken part in, or indeed heard a concert or stage performance, must have been struck by the very peculiar and most unsatisfactory end of this Act II as it stands; Aeneas sings his very beautiful recitative in A minor and disappears without any curtain music or chorus (which occurs in all the other acts). The drama cries out for some strong dramatic music, and the whole key scheme of the opera (very carefully adhered to in each of the other scenes) demands a return to the key of the beginning of the act or its relative major (D minor or F major). What is more, the contemporary printed libretto . . . has perfectly clear indications for a scene with the Sorceress and her Enchantresses, consisting of six lines of verse, and a dance to end the act. It is my considered opinion that music was certainly composed to this scene and has been lost. It is quite possible that it will be found, but each year makes it less likely.

CHP

Britten's solution was to turn the first four lines of verse into a trio for the Sorceress and two witches based on a trio from *The Indian Queen* (*c.* 1690) transposed to D minor; the last two lines became a chorus to music borrowed from the last of the nine *Welcome Songs* (1687) transposed to D major; and the dance was set to a movement in F major from the Overture to *Sir Anthony Love* (1690). (Similarly for the Mermaid Theatre productions of 1951, 1952, and 1953, Geraint Jones drew music for the missing chorus and dance from other Purcell works.)

It is at this point that *The Loves of Dido and Aeneas* as printed in the *Measure for Measure* quarto provides fresh evidence of what may have been the contemporary solution of this problem. After the passage of Aeneas's recitative ending

> Yours be the Blame, ye Gods, for I,
> Obey your will—but with more ease cou'd dye

come four lines, also for Aeneas, each of which is introduced with double quotation marks, showing they were to be omitted in performance and, presumably, not to be set to music.

> "Direct me, friends, what Choice to make,
> "Since Love and Fame together press me,
> "And with equal Force distress me.
> "Say what Party I shall take.

Here follows a duet for two friends of Aeneas, which does not appear in the original libretto. There is an occasional interjection by Aeneas, which almost raises the status of this musical number from that of a duet to a trio. Dramatically it is of considerable importance, as it emphasizes the difficult nature of the choice with which Aeneas is faced and gives it appropriate musical form. (Attention is drawn to the fact

that, apart from the quatrain for Aeneas given above, no
further lines are marked for omission.)

1 *Fr.* Resistless *Jove* Commands—
2 *Fr.* But Love
   More Resistless then *Jove's.*
Aen. But Fame *Alcander.*
2 *Fr.* Fame's a Bubble,
   Honour but a Glorious Trouble,
   A vain Pride of Destroying,
   Alarming and Arming,
   And Toiling and Moiling,
   And never Enjoying.
1 *Fr.* 'Twas that gave *Hector,*
2 *Fr.* What?
1 *Fr.* Renown and Fame.
2 *Fr.* An empty Name,
   And Lamentable Fate.
1 *Fr.* 'Twas Noble and Brave.
2 *Fr.* 'Twas a Death for a Slave.
1 *Fr.* His Valour and Glory
   Shall flourish in Story.
2 *Fr.* While he rots in his Grave.
Aen. Ye Sacred Powers instruct me how to choose,
   When Love or Empire I must loose.
Aen. & Cho. Love without Empire Triffling is and Vain,
   And Empire without Love a Pompous Pain.

                                   Exeunt.

At this point comes the stage direction '*Enter Sorceress and
Witches*', and the chorus 'Then since our Charmes have Sped'
follows as in the original 1689 libretto.

It is interesting to find this duet/trio introduced at this
particular spot. As it does not appear in the original libretto
and as the two extra men's voices would have been in-
convenient for the original girls' school production, it

is likely that Tate either suppressed this passage in 1689 or added it specially for the professional performance in 1700. It helps to give musical density to Aeneas, who in the school production was a light-weight character, confined to recitative; and it is a complete vindication of Britten's inspired guess that the exigencies of musical form called for some sort of ensemble at this point.

The only other important textual change in the libretto of *Dido and Aeneas* as printed in the 1700 quarto comes in the fourth entertainment. This is substantially the same as the classical-pastoral prologue of Tate's original libretto; but the material is slightly rearranged, the final duet between a country shepherd and shepherdess with chorus being moved to an earlier position immediately following Venus's couplet

> Smiling Hours are now before you,
> Hours that may return no more.

After the chorus ending

> Prepare those soft returns to Meet,
> That makes Loves Torments Sweet.

the Nymphs' Dance is cut, and in place of the removed duet there is a new episode—a duet between Mars and Peace with antiphonal choruses supplied by their attendants. This provides a much stronger ending, in the classical as opposed to the pastoral vein. The new material runs as follows:

> *Enter* Mars *and his Attendants, on one side,* Peace *and her Train on the other.*

Mar. Bid the Warlike Trumpet sound
Conquest waits with Lawrel crown'd,
Conquest is the Hero's due.
Glorious Triumph will ensue.

Peace. 'Tis time for War's alarms to cease,
  And Heroes crown'd with spoils,
  Enjoy the Harvest of their toils,
  And reap the happy Fruits of Peace.
Mar. & his Train *Cho.* No, no! the love would have it so
  Fame and Honour answer—No.
Peace. Wherefore must the Warriour be
  To restless Tasks assign'd,
  Give others those delights which he
  Must never hope to find,
  Shall he, whose valour gain'd
  The Prize in rough alarms,
  Be still condemn'd to arms,
  And from a Victors share detain'd.
Mar. Cho. Yes, yes.
Peace. Cho. No, no.
Mar. Cho. Fame, fame will have it so.
Peace. Cho. Love and Reason answer no.
Peace. Must he with endless toils be prest,
  Nor with repose himself be blest,
  Who gives the weary Nations rest.
Mar. Cho. Yes, yes.
Peace. Cho. No, no.
All. Love, Reason, Honour, all will have it so.
Cho. Since it is decreed that Wars should cease,
  Let's all agree to welcome Peace.

    The grand Dance.

In considering the problem of whether or not another composer was called in to complete the score in 1700, one should remember that the full description of these entertainments as given at the head of the first is '*The Loves of Dido and Aeneas, a Mask, in Four Musical Entertainments*'. There is no suggestion that any part of the text of these entertainments, with the exception of the four lines in the Grove scene that were specially marked for omission, was not set to music. Furthermore, the Prologue to *Measure for Measure*, which was written by John Oldmixon and spoken by Betterton, goes out of its way to mention by name and pay homage to the composer. At first Betterton chides the audience for their fickle attendance at the Lincoln's Inn Fields Theatre:

> To please this Winter, we all Meanes have us'd;
> Old Playes have been Reviv'd, and New produc'd.
> But you, it seems, by Us, wou'd not be Serv'd;
> And others Thrive, while we were almost Starv'd. . . .

After continuing in this vein for some time, he comes to a close; and a stage direction makes it clear he is about to make his exit when, suddenly remembering something he'd forgotten, he comes back and delivers this final triplet:

> Hold; I forgot the Business of the Day;
> No more than this, We, for our Selves, need Say,
> 'Tis *Purcels* Musick, and 'tis *Shakespears* Play.

Here is as clear an indication as possible that Purcell was fully accepted as the composer of the music to these particular entertainments.

As against this, however, the Tenbury MS. has no music for the Prologue at all, and in the Grove scene the music stops dead after Aeneas's final line of recitative, being followed by the scribe's subscription 'The End of the 2d Act'. This comes on a recto sheet; and the Prelude to the third act follows on the verso. Clearly the copyist had no suspicion that there was any gap in the music at this point. This might be accounted for by the fact that the extra music for the trio/duet and chorus, having been written by another hand, was inserted into Purcell's original score for purposes of theatrical performance, but withdrawn before the score was handed over to the copyist.

But if Purcell was not the composer of the missing parts of the score, who in fact was?

There seems to be no need to look outside the Purcell family for an answer. Since Henry's death in 1695, Daniel Purcell had been much preoccupied with composition for the stage. In the first place, he wrote the music for a masque of Hymen to complete his brother's score for *The Indian Queen*. In 1696 he set the lyrical passages in an extraordinary dramatic concoction written by George Powell and John Verbruggen and produced at Dorset Garden. This was called *Brutus of Alba*. Part of the action was based on Tate's earlier tragedy of the same name; but it also had passages of dynastic pageantry recalling *Albion and Albanius* (1685) of Grabu and Dryden, and various *commedia dell'arte* episodes. The following year (1697) he composed music for another dramatic opera, *Cinthia and Endimion*, written by D'Urfey and produced at Drury Lane. In 1698 he set an ode by Tate entitled *Lamentation on the Death of Henry Purcell*, and in the same year provided incidental music for a tragedy of Gildon's entitled *Phaeton*. In the latter case, the playwright was so delighted by the composer's contribution that he wrote a special encomium in the preface to the printed text:

... But the *Music* was so admirable, that the best Judges tell me (for I dare not give it as my own bare Sentiment) that there is the true *Purcellian Air* through the whole: that tho' it be so very different in the several Acts, it is every where Excellent; and that Mr. *Daniel Purcell*s Composition in this Play is a certain Proof, that as long as he lives Mr. *Henry Purcel* will never die; or our English harmony give place to any of our Neighbours.

Only a few weeks before the production of *Measure for*

Measure in 1700, the dramatic opera *The Grove* had its first performance at Drury Lane with music by Daniel Purcell to a libretto by Oldmixon.

All these close links with the librettist of *Dido and Aeneas* and the author of its Epilogue, and with the adapter of *Measure for Measure* and the author of its Prologue, make it evident that if extra music had been needed for *The Loves of Dido and Aeneas*, Daniel Purcell was the most likely person to be asked. Furthermore, it seems that the setting of Tate's masque-like prologue (whether in whole or in part) would have been particularly congenial to him, since in 1700 he decided to enter for a competition that had just been announced in the *London Gazette* with four prizes of 100, 50, 30, and 20 guineas for the best settings of Congreve's masque *The Judgment of Paris*, and in due course won the third prize, his version being presented, first on its own, and then with the other three winning scores, at Dorset Garden in 1701. One should also bear in mind that it was doubtless from the Purcell family—probably from the widow herself—that the management of the Lincoln's Inn Fields Theatre acquired the score of *Dido and Aeneas* for their 1700 production; and that would have made it easy for Daniel Purcell to have access to it.

Apart from the two passages quoted above, the 1700 text does not contain any new material. It corrects many of the misprints and errors in the 1689 edition, but adds a few of its own. The opening number of Act III, 'Come away Fellow-Saylors', is ascribed to the Sorceress and not to the Chorus as in the 1689 libretto or the 1st Sailor as in the Tenbury MS. (It is interesting to find the 1700 text prints the fourth line of this number as 'Take a Bouze short; leave your Nymphs on the Shore' instead of the Tenbury MS. 'Take a boozy short leave of your nymphs of the shore', which sounds as if it had been deliberately altered by Purcell for the sake of melodic euphony.) The number of dances is reduced from seventeen to ten, the display of the dancers' talents being no longer so important a factor as it had been at Priest's School in 1689.

Although the 1700 quarto gives the *Measure for Measure* cast, it says nothing about the cast for *The Loves of Dido and Aeneas*. In this connexion, a document from the Sackville (Knole) MSS. quoted by Sybil Rosenfeld in an article on 'Unpublished Stage Documents'[1] is of importance. It mentions the Lincoln's Inn Fields Company as containing on 20 July 1695 fifteen actors and a dozen actresses, and in addition:

Mr Downes	Prompter
Mr Prince ⎱	Dancers
Mr Bray ⎰	
Mr Pate ⎱	
Mr Reading ⎬	Singers
Mrs Hodgson ⎰	
The 4 Scene Keepers	

Mrs. Hodgson, who played Aglaia in *The Loves of Mars and Venus*, a play set to music by G. Finger and Eccles and inserted into Edward Ravenscroft's farce *The Anatomist* (Lincoln's Inn Fields, 1696), was certainly still in the company during the 1699-1700 season; and it seems not unreasonable to think she may have sung the role of Dido. The only other likely candidate was the actress Mrs. Bracegirdle, whose singing was specially singled out for praise by John Downes in *Roscius Anglicanus* (1708); but as she was cast for Isabella in *Measure for Measure*, it would have been physically impossible for her to have sung Dido as well. It appears from an advertisement in the *Daily Courant* that

[1] *Theatre Notebook*, Vol. XI, 1956-7.

Mrs. Hodgson sang at Lincoln's Inn Fields on 23 March
1704; so there is good reason to think that she also appeared
as Dido in the 1704 revival. As for the men, both Mr.
Reading and Mr. Pate had sung in *The Fairy Queen*, so
they were familiar with Purcell's operatic idiom. Mr. Pate,
however, was with the Drury Lane company early in 1699,
when he and Leveridge sang a dialogue in the third act of
The Island Princess; and four seasons later he was still a
member of the same company, as appears from a Drury
Lane announcement dated 11 February 1703 advertising
'an extraordinary Consort of Musick by the best Masters in
which Mr. Pate (having recover'd his Voice) will perform
several songs in Italian and English'. So perhaps it was Mr.
Reading who was cast as Aeneas.

The extra music that was used in *The Loves of Dido and
Aeneas* in 1700 does not appear to have survived. It is even
doubtful whether it was carried over into the 1704 revivals,
for there is no trace of any consciousness on the part of the
Tenbury MS. scribe that there were omissions in the score
from which he was copying. It is always possible that this
extra music may turn up; but the likelihood now seems
rather remote. Meanwhile, any modern edition of the
opera (such as Britten's) that attempts to fill the gaps in the
score as it has come down to us with appropriate music by
Purcell is to be welcomed as a step towards the fuller
realization of the true nature of the operatic masterpiece that
Tate and Purcell planned and created together.

4

Purcell's Librettist, Nahum Tate

IMOGEN HOLST

No one writing about Purcell's dramatic music can escape mentioning the fact that he never wrote another real opera after *Dido and Aeneas*. The statement has been made over and over again, in tones varying from mild regret to passionate vexation. In an article written in 1927 for *The Heritage of Music* my father even went so far as to say that it was a 'crime' for which Purcell had not been sufficiently blamed. But it is surely a little hard to blame a composer for having to earn enough to live on. Opera in seventeenth-century England was no more a paying proposition than it is today. 'Ah, Mony, Mony!' sighs the writer of the Prologue to D'Avenant's *Siege of Rhodes*, and his words have a familiar ring, in spite of their period flavour, when he goes on to wish that his patrons would

> half that Treasure spare,
> Which Faction gets from Fools to nourish War.

Audiences in the sixteen-nineties wanted stage plays with 'Singing, Dancing and Machines interwoven with 'em', and theatrical managers gave them what they were used to, steering a safe middle course and taking it for granted that the general public were not able to digest an entire opera. If *Dido and Aeneas* had not been commissioned for a private performance by amateurs it might never have been written:

it had to be disguised as a series of interludes for its first public performance on the professional stage in 1700.

Purcell's 'crime' was that he agreed to make the best of a bad job, giving his audiences a taste of opera 'to try their Palats' by providing superb incidental music for more than forty plays that were soon to be swept aside and forgotten.

The operatic societies who now give concert performances of the musical interludes in *The Fairy Queen*, *King Arthur*, and *Dioclesian* must feel frustrated almost beyond endurance when they have to stand stock still during scenes that are meant to be acted. Yet stage productions can be just as frustrating, owing to the lack of unity in the works.

The astonishing unity of *Dido and Aeneas* is often mentioned, but Tate's share in it has seldom been acknowledged. He was Purcell's only real librettist in our sense of the word. If we could find his first rough draft of the libretto of *Dido*, with Purcell's comments in the margin, it might prove almost as revealing as the discovery of the lost autograph score of the music.

In planning the work as a whole, and dividing it into scenes, Tate and Purcell must surely have been influenced by what they remembered of Blow's *Venus and Adonis*. There are the obvious resemblances, such as in the final chorus of mourning Cupids and in the dialogue between the hero and heroine, where he protests that he has changed his mind and will stay with her, and she drives him away against her own inclination. There are the same swift changes of mood, when one scene leads straight to the next with a suddenness that some twentieth-century critics still find too abrupt. And there is the same admirable directness in the choice of words.

It would be easy to fall into the temptation of thinking that Tate might have had a hand in the libretto of *Venus and*

Adonis, since he was collaborating with Blow in 1679. But there is no evidence for this. What is certain, from the evidence of *Dido*, is that Tate knew what was wanted in a libretto. He had learnt that music was 'the exaltation of poetry', and, unlike Dryden, he felt no need to complain about having to cramp his verses or to apologize for having to make his art subservient to Purcell's.

If we pour scorn on his lines and describe them as flat-footed or naïve it is because we are not equipped with enough musical imagination to realize their possibilities. We are inclined to condemn the words of the Prologue to *Dido* just because we have no tune to fit them to while we are reading them:

> See the Spring in all her Glory,
> Welcome Venus to the shore,
> Smiling Hours are now before you,
> Hours that may return no more.

Without any music the lines seem only half alive. But it would be just as mistaken to complain that they are in-adequate as it would be to complain about the apparent banality of the lines for Aeneas' first entry:

Belinda. See, your Royal Guest appears
    How God-like is the Form he bears.
Aeneas. When, Royal Fair, shall I be blest,
    With cares of Love and State distrest?
Dido. Fate forbids what you Ensue.
Aeneas. Aeneas has no Fate but you.
    Let Dido smile, and I'le defie
    The Feeble Stroke of Destiny.

In these eight lines the music exalts the libretto, but it is the libretto that has brought the music into being.

On the professional stage this first entry of the hero would

have had all the splendour of a flourish of trumpets. But
there was no money to spare for trumpets—and probably
no room for them, either—in Mr. Priest's School at Chelsea,
so Belinda conveys the excitement of a fanfare in the actual
notes of her recitative:

Ex. 1

Purcell's extraordinary power of dramatic characterization
can be recognized in the very first words that Aeneas sings;
faced with having to make a proposal of marriage in public,
the god-like Prince of Troy is as tongue-tied as any reticent
Englishman; he is so overcome by emotion that he begins
his recitative too low down and has to start again, a fourth
higher. When Dido tells him that Fate is against them he
immediately becomes more confident: as a soldier, he feels
on firmer ground with an enemy to face. There is the
gesture of a drawn sword in his rising phrase: it is strength-
ened by the wide-mouthed, bright insistence of the repeated
vowel 'i' in the line

Let Dido smile and I'le defie,

where Purcell seizes on what would be considered a weakness in poetry and triumphantly turns it to musical advantage:

The phrase is a wonderful example of Purcell's 'genius for expressing the energy of English words'; after the climax of 'defie', the word 'feeble' sinks down with no strength left in its curving spinelessness; the 'k' of 'stroke' cuts across the cadence like a knife; while in the final word 'destiny', the hero conveys his scorn in the low level of his voice, yet, at the same time the harmonic resolution makes it quite clear to the listener that Fate is going to have the last word in the tragedy that is beginning to unfold.

Tate must have learned a good deal from his adaptations of Shakespeare, for, in his libretto for Purcell, he was able to reach beyond the physical barrier of the three walls of the stage, particularly at the unforgettable moment when the Sorceress and her witches hear the distant sound of the royal hunt. It is interesting to compare his original lines with the even more dramatic version that Purcell has made of the words.

Tate wrote:

> The Queen and He are now in Chase,
> Hark, how the cry comes on apace.
> But when they've done, &c.

The word 'how' suggests that he thought that the first sound of the distant hunt would be heard at the end of that line. But by cutting out the 'how', Purcell was able to give his pianissimo strings their first horn-call *before* the isolated 'Hark!'

In the Grove scene, the sense of approaching disaster is already suggested in the libretto, with its references to the tragic fates of Actaeon and Adonis. And, in the last act, when the disaster is reached, Tate never for an instant allows the two lovers to utter any of the conventional platitudes that would have transformed them into puppets. He has been ridiculed for giving Dido such unexpected lines as:

> Thus on the fatal Banks of Nile,
> Weeps the deceitful Crocodile.

But it is brilliant characterization. For Dido is obviously working herself up into a state: Cleopatra and other desperate Queens have done the same sort of thing when the occasion has arisen. The fact that Aeneas gives way to her makes matters worse, for she begins nagging him. 'I'm now resolved as well as you' has the brittle self-assertion of one whose nerves are strained beyond control.

The quarrel is so dramatically convincing that it is almost too painful to listen to, especially when Dido is driven to the fatal feminine weakness of saying: ' 'Tis enough . . . that you had once a thought of leaving me.' It is this that makes the entry of the chorus at 'Great minds against themselves conspire' one of the most moving moments in the whole work. Even the 'remember me' of the Lament owes some of its poignancy to the way in which Dido's creators, throughout the opera, have made her unforgettable as a person. Every detail has helped, including that much-maligned crocodile. And Tate must have his share of the glory.

5

Our Sense of Continuity in English Drama and Music

MICHAEL TIPPETT

When considering the heritage of our musical past it is clear enough that we are contemplating a continuity, but it is also clear that the continuity works by fits and starts. This is so whether we think of ourselves as Europeans or as English.

Although the rediscovery of Bach's music seems to have been initially an accident, the tremendous and world-wide revival has implied a general need to feed into the present a music of the past; but a music which at Bach's death was being forgotten and rejected as old-fashioned. This is an example of what I mean by continuity by fits and starts.

I regard the revival of Purcell as less important than the revival of Bach, but it is a revival of the same kind. We are now in a period when music of the generation before Bach, the music of Schütz and Purcell—and even of the generation earlier, the music of Monteverdi—is being revived to meet some need of our time. But as before, with the music of Bach, it is only gradually that the revival spreads from the enthusiasts and the small societies to the general public. And, as before, it is not easy to make music of so distant a past fit into the concerts of our day.

If through this revival Purcell's music becomes a living though small part of our general European heritage (for among English composers only Purcell can be said to belong to a *living* European continuity), it must form a very important part indeed of our local English heritage. This is not only because of the lack of great names in English musical history, but also because of the spoken language. By this I do not mean so much the obvious fact that music to English texts is naturally closer to English singers; I mean that certain things in Purcell's setting of English words are vital to English composers. For, more than anyone else, the creative artist needs a sense of continuity.

Now it can be said that in English poetry the heritage is the richest, in English painting the poorest; and in English music the heritage falls in between and is the least explored —that is explored in the sense that English poetry is always being explored and revalued. Only English folk-song, Tudor music, and the music of Purcell have so far given the vital sense of continuity to latter-day English composers. And if the generation older than my own has more fully explored folk-song and Tudor music, my own generation has more fully explored the music of Purcell. And it is also our later generation that has come to maturity at a time when, at last, there are regularly functioning English opera houses in the capital. This makes it possible for our sense of continuity with Purcell to be helpful in the writing of opera. I think this is indeed so; though not by any implied and thoughtless equation of Purcell with opera. The period of the most vital English theatre is clearly Elizabethan, not Restoration. The period of the most vital English opera productions is the eighteenth century,— the period from Gay, Arne, Handel, to the London Bach.

It is a commonplace that while the Elizabethan composers wrote music almost exclusively for the church and the house, the Restoration composers wrote for the church and the theatre. As to Purcell we can say that his public musical life is triangular, stretched out between church, theatre, and court. His church music follows on directly from that of Gibbons with one significant difference. Gibbons, grounded on Tallis and Byrd, wrote full verse anthems, as Purcell did after him, but Gibbons was still part and parcel of the church musical reform which substituted English for Latin, and insisted on the strict rule of one syllable to a note. It took virtually two generations of English composers to carry this out, but by the time Gibbons died the work was complete.

At the same time the shape of anthems was changing; the accompanied verse anthem reaching out towards the cantata. And here the work of reform was not complete.

When Purcell began to compose his church music, the English language, as opposed to Latin, was already the normal one, but for his purposes it was unduly restricted to an old rule of syllable-to-a-note; while the verse anthem as handed down from Gibbons was formal, stiff, and contrapuntally too intricate to satisfy him. In the matter of the English language Purcell broke away from the old syllabic rule, and wrote, when he wanted, coloratura for English words. This was a decisive change of practice. And in the matter of the changing forms he learnt to dramatize the verse anthem in a way denied to Gibbons. This can be seen in an instant by comparing 'This is the Record of John' with 'My Beloved spake'.

It is not that Purcell was any more alive to the English language than Tallis, Byrd, or Gibbons. If we believed that, it would be as if we failed to see the beauty of a dumpy Elizabethan tune like 'O Mistress mine' because it hasn't the carry of 'Lilliburlero'. It is a different beauty arising from a different purpose. The demands of the second Stuart court and capital were for a civic music with all the elegance, frankness, and immediacy of Restoration manners. The only effective style at hand was an English version of that which the Italian-born Lully had invented for Le Roi Soleil. The Odes for St. Cecilia's Day and the Birthday and Welcome Odes form Purcell's legacy in this genre. The demands of the theatre were for an unending stream of rapidly-composed incidental music; overtures, dances, songs, dramatic monologues, choruses, and indeed all the ingredients of opera, though never the opera proper. *Dioclesian, The Fairy Queen, King Arthur, The Indian Queen,* and the rest of the long list bear witness to Purcell's industry in providing the unending stream.

It is unthinkable that composers of my generation, caught up in, if not actual instigators of, the general revival of Purcell's music, should not feel a special sense of continuity with this Restoration composer. Failing an English opera composer as such, Purcell is all that there is. His dramatic music, though incidental, is wonderful in its own right. The general style of his time had loosened the approach to the language, and Purcell had the great gift to make full use of this new freedom, without ever departing from the absolutely natural technique of setting English to music, which had been handed on by the Elizabethans. So that Purcell offers us something the Elizabethans did not possess at all. By the time the next great composer of English is writing, that is to say with the production of Handel's oratorios, the whole scene has undergone another decisive change, because Italian has become the universal language for opera; and the English ballad opera has nothing to offer us here. So Purcell stands at the only possible moment in English musical history when a genius could have done what he did. Since he was this genius our sense of continuity with him, in respect of incidental music for the English theatre, is vital.

There is a point to make here before we proceed. It must not be thought that Purcell used only coloratura in the setting of English. When he needed to do so he could set words in as simple a manner as Gibbons. One has only to think of the sustained line of Dido's Lament. The setting of Tate's words is as uncomplicated as anything from the earlier age. But what is unique is the placing and the timing. The key-word 'remember' is not only used magnificently for the sake of its own verbal rhythm, but is repeated and placed in such a way as to give the greatest sense of sustained passion and climax. The nearest approach to this in music from the earlier age would be some of the monologues of Dowland. But Dowland's is basically private grief, and Purcell's is public and theatrical.

With the single exception of *Dido and Aeneas* which is a true opera, Purcell's music for the theatre is incidental. It offers, as I said before, all the ingredients of opera, but the theatrical pieces for which it was written were not operas. That is to say that Purcell's relations with the dramatists were never those of composer to librettist. From this it follows that while Purcell's dramatic music provides us with the only exhaustive compendium of musical techniques for use in the English theatre, it does not provide us with any models for that unification of drama with musical technique which we call opera. From every point of view this is a loss; but it is as well to be quite clear about it.

Part of what this loss means can be gauged, I think, by following a line of thought suggested by a modern poet-dramatist, T. S. Eliot, concerning Shakespeare. The matter I have in mind appears near the beginning of his published essay *Poetry and Drama*. Eliot wants to abstract a dramatic element and a musical element from within the unified verse play; and then to consider how the pattern of drama and the pattern of music (the music of poetry of course, not of playing or singing) has been correlated by the genius of the poet-dramatist—a practice very similar to the ideal collaboration of composer with librettist. To exemplify his argument Eliot analyses the 'opening scene of *Hamlet*— as well constructed an opening scene as that of any play ever written—which has the advantage of being one that everybody knows'. Eliot's analysis of the *Hamlet* scene often reads nearly like a figurative analysis of a piece of music. To give an extreme example; Eliot writes: 'It would be interesting to pursue . . . this problem of the double pattern in great poetic drama—the pattern which may be examined from the point of view of stagecraft or from that of the music.' By reading 'opera' for 'poetic drama', the word 'music' will have the sense in which a composer uses it, not a poet.

I have begun with this extreme example because it shows the deceptive ease with which one may equate verse-drama to opera. As the danger of consequent misunderstanding is real, I should like, before pursuing the *Hamlet* analysis, to make my position clear.

I take Suzanne Langer's common-sense view that 'Every work [of art] has its being in only one order of art; compositions of different orders are not simply conjoined, but all except one will cease to appear as what they are'. This principle is a vital one and needs to be understood as it works out in practice. So I quote from Langer's exposition of what happens to plastic art and to music when used as accessories in a stage play. She says:

Drama . . . swallows all plastic creations that enter into its theatrical precinct, and their own pictorial, architectural, or sculptural beauties do not add themselves to its own beauty.

A great work of sculpture, say the original Venus of Milo, transported to the comic or the tragic stage would count only as a stage setting, an element in the action and might not meet this purpose as well as a pasteboard counterfeit of it would do.

And

A song sung on the stage in a good play is a piece of dramatic action. If we receive it in the theatre as we would receive it in a concert, the play is a pastiche.

I think Langer states the fundamentals very clearly. If, e.g., the order of the work of art is that of a play, then the drama proper will eat up stage settings and music and even poetry in order to present us with a play, not an opera.

The complementary process Langer sums up neatly in one phrase: 'Music ordinarily swallows words and action creating [thereby] opera, oratorio or song.'

If we keep these *primal* distinctions in mind, we can pursue profitably I think the analogies that do really exist between verse-drama and opera. So that we can follow Eliot's analysis of the *Hamlet* scene with an eye to considering what can be learnt from it as to the double pattern of drama and music—always keeping in mind that music in a verse-drama is the music of poetry, and is to be eaten up by the drama; while music in an opera is the music of instruments and voices and is to swallow the drama.

The analysis begins:

From the short, brusque ejaculations at the beginning, suitable to the situation and to the character of the guards . . . the verse glides into a slower movement with the appearance of the courtiers Horatio and Marcellus.

Horatio says *'Tis but our fantasy* . . . and the movement changes again on the appearance of Royalty, the ghost of the King, into the solemn and sonorous *What art thou, that usurp'st this time of night* . . . There is an abrupt change to staccato in Horatio's words to the Ghost on its second appearance; this rhythm changes again with the words

> *We do it wrong, being so majestical*
> *To offer it a show of violence . . .*

The scene reaches a resolution with the words of Marcellus:

> *It faded on the crowing of the cock . . .*

Because of the use of words like 'slower movement' and 'staccato' this reads like the analysis of the opening scene of an opera, if we have deliberately turned our attention to that possibility. This analysis of Eliot's, which I have of course curtailed, aims at making us see how the movement of the drama between the characters of the guards, the courtiers, and the ghost, is matched by a movement of the nature and speed of the verse—just as in an operatic scene it is matched by the nature and speed of the music.

When Horatio says:

> But look, the morn, in russet mantle clad,
> Walks o'er the dew of yon high eastern hill.
> Break we our watch up.

Eliot observes: 'This is great poetry, and it is dramatic; but besides being poetic and dramatic it is something more.' It is verse-drama. It is opera!

There emerges, when we analyse it, a kind of musical design also, which reinforces and is one with the dramatic movement. It has checked and accelerated the pulse of our emotion without our knowing it.

This would be ideal opera!

Note that in these last words of Marcellus there is a deliberate brief emergence of the poetic into consciousness.

A *scena* in *recitativo strumentato* goes over for a moment into *arioso*.

When we hear the lines

> *But look, the morn, in russet mantle clad,*
> *Walks o'er the dew of yon high eastern hill*

we are lifted for a moment beyond character, but with no sense of unfitness of the words coming, and at this moment, from the lips of Horatio.

What an example for the timing and placing of the *arioso* within the *scena*!

The transitions in the scene obey laws of the music of dramatic poetry.

Or if we rewrite the sentence: The transitions in the scene obey laws of the natural movement of dramatic music.

Eliot's point is that only a master like Shakespeare can so correlate the pattern of the drama with the pattern of the music of the poetry that they are indistinguishable; and so create that something extra, which, if taken into music-drama, we call great opera. Purcell, the master of dramatic music, was only once in a position to create this true correlation of the two patterns. This was in *Dido and Aeneas*. What he was asked to do on other occasions can be seen in the music for *The Fairy Queen*; a set of five unrelated masques, or *divertissements*, interlarded with a hotch-potch version of *A Midsummer Night's Dream*. Therefore it is useless for us to go to Purcell for the secrets of the true correlation of music and drama even though he is the unique master of English dramatic music for the theatre. We should do better, even if we are composers not poets, to go to Shakespeare, and to pursue throughout whole plays the kind of analysis which Eliot has made of one scene. If we were skilled enough, as a poet might be, to disentangle the musical pattern of the verse in order to lay it alongside the correlative pattern of the drama between the characters, we might find that living continuity of our heritage which we cannot hope to find in Purcell's incidental music owing to its unavoidable limitations.

The continuity with Shakespeare has never depended on a revival in the manner of the present revival of interest in Purcell. But I think it true to say that the deeper insights into Shakespeare's art as a verse-dramatist, which we owe to the successful verse-dramatists of our own time, are quite new. I am suggesting that the English composer might be able to profit by these new insights to procure for himself one of the elements necessary to a sense of continuity of English opera, but generally missing from Purcell, the element of the double pattern of drama and music. But because this element in Shakespeare is only exemplified in verse-drama and not in opera proper, a composer has always to translate these insights into other terms, and, obviously enough, the Shakespearian drama does not provide that compendium of dramatic music for the English theatre which Purcell's works alone provide.

It is a strange sense of continuity that has its elements so divided in time and manner. Yet if it is really possible that the English composer can see how to use Shakespeare as the master for certain things that are usually only sought for in great operatic composers as such, then our sense of musical continuity with Purcell may be further developed and fructified.

6

Purcell and the Chapel Royal

JEREMY NOBLE

More than a hundred years ago Purcell's church music was published in a practically complete, if not very accurate, edition by Vincent Novello, yet it remains less well known as a whole than any other branch of his output. Even in our more enterprising cathedral and collegiate churches the number of Purcell's anthems in regular use is deplorably small. There are various reasons for this, both of taste and of technical difficulty. The frank directness with which Purcell translates the joy or the grief of the Psalmist into the current musical terms of his own day is felt by some people to be too secular, too theatrical, but although no one in his senses would claim that Purcell's church music expressed a spiritual experience as profound or intense as that of Byrd or Bach, it is certainly less superficial than that of many composers who figure prominently in cathedral music-lists, and as music infinitely more rewarding. As for the charge that it is too difficult for the average choir, this sounds more like an excuse than a reason, when 'average choirs' can hardly be restrained from tackling the much more difficult music of Bach and Handel. In the near future the Purcell Society will complete its authoritative edition of the church music; the present article is intended as a brief footnote to it—and an encouragement not to allow the forthcoming volumes to gather dust on their purchasers' shelves.

As a child Purcell was one of the twelve choristers of the Chapel Royal, and at the age of twenty-three he followed his father and his uncle in being appointed a Gentleman. With twelve boys and thirty-two men (even though some of the latter can have attended only rarely) the Chapel Royal was the most sumptuous ecclesiastical establishment in the country, and there is no reason to doubt that all of Purcell's church music was at some time performed by it, even though some of the simpler pieces may have been written with the capabilities of smaller choirs, such as that of Westminster Abbey, in mind. Quite apart from the interest that naturally attaches to an institution with which Purcell was so closely connected there is, therefore, the possibility that the following brief account of the Chapel Royal in his day may clarify some problems of performance.

The list on page 55 of the Gentlemen of the Chapel Royal who were in office during Purcell's own period as a Gentleman (i.e. from July 1682 to November 1695) has been compiled mainly from information in the Old Cheque-Book, a comprehensive register kept by one of the Gentlemen known as the Clerk of the Cheque, to record such matters as appointments, admonitions, and petitions. The Old Cheque-Book was published by E. F. Rimbault in 1872 for the Camden Society (New Series, III); by kind permission of the Sub-Dean of the Chapel Royal, Rimbault's edition has been compared with the original manuscript, still kept at St. James's Palace, and it has also been supplemented from other sources. The list is arranged in chronological order of appointment and divided into four groups: (*a*) those whose musical careers we know to have begun before the Commonwealth, even though they may not have been appointed to the Chapel until the Restoration; (*b*) the remainder of the Gentlemen who were appointed to the reconstituted Chapel in 1660 and the beginning of 1661; (c) those appointed between the Restoration and Purcell's own appointment; (d) those appointed during his thirteen years as a Gentleman to fill vacant places. Groups (a), (b), and (c) taken together thus show the constitution of the Chapel just before Purcell entered it; Edward Lowe, to whose place he succeeded, has been included. Dates in brackets indicate 'extraordinary', i.e. unpaid, appointments as recorded in the Cheque-Book; these were sometimes made for a particular occasion, sometimes as a first step to an 'ordinary' place, and where a bracketed date is not followed by an unbracketed one it is to be assumed that full membership of the Chapel was not granted. In these cases the second column of dates—departure from the Chapel— obviously does not apply. The office of Gentleman of the Chapel Royal was normally held for life, and unless other- wise stated the date of 'departure' is the date of death. The type of voice—counter-tenor, tenor, or bass—is indicated by C, T, or B, and the post of organist by O.

One thing that emerges clearly from even the most cursory examination of this list of Gentlemen of the Chapel Royal is that a very high standard of professional com- petence must have been maintained. For a brief period after the Restoration it seemed an almost impossible task to repair the loss of traditional skill caused by sixteen years' interrup- tion of the musical services, and the preface to Edward Lowe's *A Short Direction for the Performance of Cathedrall Service* (1661; 2nd ed., 1664) reflects the anxiety of the older generation of church musicians. But by 1682 the position had improved immeasurably. For one thing, there were still a number of musicians to provide continuity with the pre- Commonwealth period. It was the death of Lowe, organist of Christ Church, Oxford, since the 1630s, that provided a

GENTLEMEN OF THE CHAPEL ROYAL, 1682-95

		Admitted	Died
(a)	John Harding	B 1638	7 Nov. 1684
	Thomas Blagrave	C 1660/1	21 Nov. 1688
	Dr. William Child	O 1660/1[1]	23 (24?) Mar. 1697[2]
	Edward Lowe	O 1660/1	11 July 1682
(b)	George Bettenham	B 1660/1	19 Sept. 1694
	Edward Braddock	T 1660/1	12 June 1708
	James Cobb	T 1660/1	20 July 1697
	Henry Frost	T 1660/1	after 11 April 1689
	John Goodgroome	C 1660/1	27 June 1704
	Thomas Purcell	T 1660/1	31 July 1682
	Rev. John Sayer	T 1660/1	Jan. 1694
	Nathaniel Watkins	C 1660/1	8 May 1702
(c)	Rev. George Yardley	B 7 June 1662	after 23 April 1685
	Rev. Blase White	B 14 March 1664	25 Feb. 1700
	Thomas Richardson	C Aug. 1664	23 July 1712
	Rev. William Hopwood	B 25 Oct. 1664	13 July 1683
	Rev. Henry Smith	T 4 Oct. 1666	23 May 1688
	William Turner	C 11 Oct. 1669	13 June 1740
	Rev. James Hart	B 7 Nov. 1670	8 May 1718
	Richard Hart	B 26 April 1671	8 Feb. 1690
	Rev. Andrew Trebeck	B 5 Oct. 1671	19 Nov. 1715
	Rev. Stephen Crespion	—[3] 13 May 1673	25 Nov. 1711
	Dr. John Blow	O 16 March 1674	1 Oct. 1708
	Rev. William Powell	T 21 July 1674	after 23 April 1685
	Michael Wise	C 6 Jan. 1676	24 Aug. 1687
	Alphonso Marsh, jun.	T 25 April 1676	5 April 1692
	Rev. J. C. Sharole	B 26 Oct. 1676	5 Aug. 1687
	Thomas Heywood	T 29 March 1679	resigned Michaelmas, 1688
	Rev. John Gostling	B (25 Feb. 1678) Feb.-March 1678	17 July 1733
	John Abell	C (1 May 1679) Jan. 1680	dismissed 1688[4]
	Morgan Harris	T 20 Feb. 1680	2 Nov. 1697
	Rev. Leonard Woodson	B 15 Aug. 1681	14 March 1717
	HENRY PURCELL	O 14 July 1682[5]	21 Nov. 1695
(d)	Josias Boucher	C 6 Aug. 1682	6 Dec. 1695[6]
	Nathaniel Vestment	B (28 June 1683) 23 July	23 Aug. 1702
	Rev. Samuel Bentham	B (24 July 1683) 10 Nov. 1684	March 1730

		Admitted	Died
Thomas Browne	—	(1683)	—
Edward Morton	C	(12 April 1685)	—
William Davis	—	(23 May 1685)	—
John Lenton	—	(10 Nov. 1685)[7]	—
John James Gaches	—	(8 Nov. 1688)[8]	
Moses Snow	T	(17 Dec. 1689) 8 April 1692	20 Dec. 1702
Rev. Thomas Linacre	T?	(27 Dec. 1689) 2 March 1699	Aug. 1719
Alexander Damascene	C	(6 Dec. 1690) 10 Dec. 1695	14 July 1719
John Howell	C	(30 Aug. 1691) 10 Dec. 1695	15 July 1708
David la Count	—	(31 Aug. 1691)	—
William Battle	—	(10 Dec. 1691)	—
Simon Corbett	—	(11 Dec. 1691)	—
· Daniel Williams	B	(16 Dec. 1692) 1 April 1697	12 March 1720
Charles Greene	—	(2 Jan. 1693)	—
George Hart	T	(10 Sept. 1694) 9 Nov. 1697	29 Feb. 1699
Charles Barnes	C	(10 Sept. 1694) June 1696	2 Jan. 1711

NOTES

[1] Child was appointed one of the organists of St. George's Chapel, Windsor, in 1632, and is stated in *Grove* and elsewhere to have served concurrently as an organist of the Chapel Royal; there is no record in the Cheque-Book, however, of his having any official appointment in the Chapel before the Restoration.

[2] The date of Child's death is given as 24 March in the Cheque-Book, but in *Grove* as the 23rd, possibly following the inscription on his tombstone.

[3] Crespion was Confessor to the Royal Household and Precentor of Westminster Abbey, but there is nothing to show whether he sang tenor or bass in the Chapel.

[4] Abell became a member of James II's Catholic Chapel (the only Gentleman of the Chapel Royal to do so), and at the accession of William and Mary appears to have been dismissed. He certainly left the country, and did not return until 1700. He died at Cambridge in 1724.

[5] The date of the warrant for Purcell's appointment. His swearing-in did not take place until 16 September.

[6] The Cheque-Book appears to give 16 December, and Rimbault reads it so; but Boucher's successor, John Howell, was sworn in on the 10th and the '1' in the manuscript could be a blot.

[7] Lenton probably died soon after 1718, when his name disappears from the Royal Band.

[8] The Clerk of the Cheque originally wrote 'extraordinary'; the 'extra' was later crossed out, but as no further reference to Gaches occurs in the Cheque-Book it seems unlikely that he was ever appointed to full membership.

place for Purcell. John Harding, who survived for another two years, had been one of the choristers at James I's funeral in 1625 and still took an active part in the work of the Chapel, regularly attending the Court at Windsor. Blagrave, a friend of Pepys and since 1662 the Clerk of the Cheque, had entered royal service in 1638 as a member of Charles I's band of 'sackbuts and hoboys'—a group in which his father also played. He later took up the violin, and was in fact one of the founder-members of the select band of twenty-four that Charles II formed in emulation of Louis XIV. It comes as something of a shock, too, to realize that the venerable Dr. Child, who had been born in 1606, outlived Purcell by sixteen months.

Nor was Purcell alone in belonging to a family of musicians. We have already mentioned that Blagrave's father, Richard, was a member of the royal wind-music, and it seems likely that Harding was related to the James Harding who served Elizabeth and James I as a flautist. Goodgroome was probably a brother of the Theodore Goodgroome who taught Pepys and his wife singing; and the John Goodgroome who was organist of St. Peter's, Cornhill, was the son of one or the other. Alphonso Marsh's father, also Alphonso, had been one of the royal musicians since the reign of Charles I, and a Gentleman of the Chapel Royal since 1660; he had died only a year before Purcell was appointed. Thomas Heywood was almost certainly a member of the famous family of actors and musicians who had been connected with the Court for 150 years, and the Woodsons were another family who had produced at least three generations of musicians.

To a contemporary it might have seemed a lean period for composers in the Chapel, with Matthew Locke and the young Pelham Humfrey both recently dead, but a quick look reveals a number of prominent composers of church music, apart from Purcell himself: Child, William Turner, Blow, and the unfortunate Michael Wise, who rushed from his house after a quarrel with his wife and was killed by a blow on the head from a night-watchman whom he encountered. Composers of church music are only to be expected in the Chapel, but a surprising number of the Gentlemen are also represented in the song-collections of the time. Blow and James Hart were prolific song-writers, and so too were several of the younger post-Purcellian generation: John Lenton (who was one of the royal violins and wrote a considerable quantity of theatre music), Moses Snow (also a violinist and a member of the Westminster Abbey choir), and the famous French counter-tenor Damascene.

Naturally enough, the Chapel contained a number of the best singers of the time, and these are of particular interest in that they were responsible for the first performances of many of Purcell's works—not only the anthems, but also the occasional cantatas. Most of the soloists whose names have been preserved on manuscript scores of Welcome Songs and Birthday and Cecilian Odes are drawn from among the members of the Chapel. It has been conjectured that Turner's St. Cecilia Ode for 1685, 'Tune the viol', was an amateurish composition since it was never printed, but its composer was regarded as an indispensable counter-tenor soloist on these occasions. Boucher, Purcell's almost exact contemporary in the Chapel Royal, Damascene, and John Abell are also frequently specified as counter-tenor soloists, although Abell was on the Continent from about 1688 to 1700. (He had studied in Italy, and Evelyn describes him as 'that famous treble' and says of his voice that 'one would have sworn it was a woman's, it was so high and excellently managed'.) John Howell was also a high counter-tenor, and his appointment to the Chapel was probably an attempt to fill the gap in its ranks left by Abell.

Among the basses Gostling traditionally stands supreme, but we should not let his great reputation blind us to the fact that he had rivals. The extended range of Purcell's bass parts (which is considered on page 63 in another context) can hardly have been due to one man's phenomenal powers. Of the Gentlemen of the Chapel who are named as bass soloists in Purcell's Odes, Leonard Woodson and Daniel Williams appear most frequently; but the most important of Gostling's rivals was not a member of the Chapel, although he was in royal service. John Bowman, a theatre singer and member of the Private Music (as Gostling was too), must have been at the height of his powers during Purcell's lifetime, for he died in 1739 at the advanced age of eighty-eight. He was the original interpreter of the parts of Grimbald in *King Arthur* and Cardenio in *Don Quixote*, and the music Purcell wrote for him leaves no doubt that he was one of the finest singers of the age. Bowman and the counter-tenor Anthony Robert (perhaps the son of the musician of the same name who had been in charge of Henrietta Maria's music at Somerset House) are practically the only singers taking solo parts in the Odes who were not, either at the time or soon after, Gentlemen of the Chapel; both were in the Private Music, and it may have been religious reasons that prevented them from being appointed to the Chapel.

Tenor soloists play a less important part in Purcell's scheme of things than counter-tenors and basses; usually only two are named in the scores of the Odes, as against three or four of the other voices. However, among those named Alphonso Marsh appears frequently, and so do Freeman and Church, both of whom were to be appointed Gentlemen of the Chapel Royal soon after Purcell's death.

Originally there had been no specific post of organist in the Chapel Royal; organists had been drawn from among those Gentlemen with a particular aptitude for keyboard-playing. But during the seventeenth century the organists' special function came to be acknowledged officially, and from the Restoration onwards it was normal for three to hold office at any one time. Of the three organists in the period immediately before Purcell's appointment two were old men, each of them with commitments away from London—namely at Windsor and at Oxford. The main burden of their duties must have fallen on Blow, and the appointment of Purcell to the place made vacant by Edward Lowe's death would bring the two men into close co-operation. Probably Purcell was appointed more on the strength of his prowess as a keyboard-player than for his voice, for although the organists had to take their turn in the choir there is no independent evidence to suggest that any of them was well known as a singer—certainly not in the same class as those mentioned above as soloists.

Purcell's own voice has been the subject of some speculation. The *Gentleman's Journal* for November 1692 is un-equivocal in its report of the St. Cecilia Ode for that year (Purcell's own 'Hail, bright Cecilia!'):

The following Ode was admirably set to Music by Mr. *Henry Purcell*, and perform'd twice with universal applause, particularly the second Stanza ['Tis Nature's voice], which was sung with incredible Graces by Mr. *Purcell* himself.

Now presumably Motteux, or his correspondent, cannot have slipped up on so straightforward a matter of fact, yet it seems amazing that if Purcell were capable of giving a really satisfactory performance of such florid music we should hear no more of him as a singer. And although it was probably copied out for a later performance it is worth noting that Purcell's autograph score bears the name of 'Mr. Pate' against this particular verse. (Pate, who was a well-known theatre singer, was dismissed from the Playhouse company in June 1695 for his part in a Jacobite riot, and appears to have travelled abroad: Evelyn heard him on 30 May 1698, when he was 'lately come from Italy'; on this occasion he sang 'many rare Italian recitatives, &c., and several compositions of the late Mr. Purcell'.) Thus in spite of the evidence of the *Gentleman's Journal* it seems just possible that the singer of ''Tis Nature's voice' at its first performance was Pate and not Purcell. Could someone have scribbled down 'Mr. P.' in his notes and misinterpreted them when he came to write the occasion up? Any music critic could confirm that stranger things have happened.

In his admirable book on Purcell, Professor Westrup made an attempt to reconcile the presumption that he sang counter-tenor with the fact that Sandford lists him among the basses in his account of James II's coronation. But although Sandford's list is a useful guide, its purpose is primarily to tell us in what order the Gentlemen processed, rather than to give us information about their voices. For the sake of easy reference it is given here, with the spelling of the names brought into conformity with the previous list:

COUNTER-TENORS

1. (Wise)	2. (Heywood)	3. (Abell)	4. Boucher
Morton	Dr. Uvedal	Benford	
5. Turner	6. Richardson	7. Goodgroome	8. Watkins

TENORS

9. Harris	10. Marsh	11. Frost	12. Powell
13. Cobb	14. Braddock	15. (Smith)	16. Sayer
		Geo. Hart	

BASSES

17. Richard Hart	18. Bentham	19. Woodson	20. Gostling
21. Purcell	22. Vestment	23. Sharole	24. Trebeck
25. Bettenham	26. James Hart	27. White	28. Yardley
29. Blagrave	30. Staggins	31. (Blow)	32. Child
		Fra. Forcer	
	1. Crespion	2. Holder	

The numbering is Sandford's; Crespion and Holder, as Confessor and Sub-Dean, are numbered separately from the Gentlemen of the Chapel, even though the former held a Gentleman's place. The names given in brackets are those of Gentlemen unable to attend the ceremony; Sandford, it will be seen, even tells us who their deputies were. Now it is clear that the last file, immediately in front of Crespion and Holder, was made up not of basses, but of the Chapel's most important members: seniority was conferred upon Child and Blow by their doctorates, quite apart from the former's great age; Blagrave was Clerk of the Cheque and Child's closest rival in length of service; and Nicholas Staggins, though not actually a Gentleman of the Chapel, was Master of the King's Music (namely, the twenty-four violins, who would also be taking part in the ceremony), and had received a doctorate only three years earlier. Purcell was not senior enough to walk in this august group, and so he may well have been included among the basses simply to make up a complete file. At any rate, Sandford's list is insufficient evidence on which to argue that he was a capable singer in both bass and counter-tenor registers—like Mr. Pordage of the King's Catholic Chapel, who, according to Evelyn, had 'an excellent voice both treble and bass'.

In fact it seems to have been much more usual for singers to combine with the role of counter-tenor that of tenor. A perusal of the Cheque-Book shows that Thomas Richardson signed an affidavit in March 1664 in which he refers to himself as 'being to be sworn into the next place of a lay tenor or counter-tenor'; Andrew Carter in January of the same year was 'to come into pay when the next tenor or counter-tenor's place shall be void'; and Thomas Heywood, who succeeded to a counter-tenor's place and whom we see in the first file of counter-tenors in Sandford's list, was in 1685 confirmed in the Private Music as a tenor. This interchangeability of tenor and counter-tenor voices, even though it may not have been very frequently practised, does give us a clearer idea of the type of voice Purcell had in mind for his counter-tenor parts. A cursory examination of his anthems reveals that the sixteenth-century ideal of voices of equal compass equally spaced at intervals of a fourth or fifth from one another had been much modified. Purcell's counter-tenor and tenor parts have, as a rule, a compass of a ninth or a tenth in the verse sections, an octave or less in the choruses. Bass parts, on the other hand, often approach a two-octave compass, and sometimes even exceed it; this occurs too often to be attributed solely to the phenomenal range of the Rev. Mr. Gostling. Purcell's basses were evidently real basses, from whom low E's and D's could be demanded, but they must have been expected to extend their compass upwards by a discreet use of head-voice. As for the counter-tenors, it looks as though they—or at any rate the majority of those in the Chapel Royal—were more like high light tenors than purely falsetto voices, for Purcell rarely makes them go higher than B flat or B, while his tenors have an equal range about a major third lower. This would tally with his usual manner of writing for the conventional A T B trio, in which A and T move in stepwise chains of parallel thirds, while B is considerably more far-ranging and independent; the proper blend could only have been achieved if counter-tenor and tenor were similar in timbre.

An examination of the available records of the Chapel Royal also gives us some idea of the balance of forces Purcell would have regarded as normal. Although in the total muster of the Chapel basses outnumbered both tenors and counter-tenors it should be noted that they contain far more than their fair share of clergymen, not all of whom were as distinguished singers as Gostling. For practical purposes the three kinds of male voice were regarded as equivalent in weight, voice for voice; for when the Court repaired to Windsor, and the Chapel with it, it was customary for between four and six of each voice to be deputed, together with eight boys. This gives a much higher proportion of men to boys than we are accustomed to hearing nowadays, but there can be little doubt that the over-weighting of the top part so characteristic of modern church choirs is a comparatively recent innovation—due partly to a change in musical taste and partly to the increasing difficulty of maintaining a sufficient body of lay-clerks.

One of the main difficulties facing anyone who wishes today to perform Purcell's anthems in the course of a normal service is the fact that some of the best of them make use of strings—and Purcell's string-writing, as one might expect, is too idiomatic to be happily transferred to the organ. The story of Charles I's introduction of the band of violins into the Chapel services in 1662 and the scandal it caused to the more conservative musicians—and, doubtless, divines—has often been narrated, but it is sometimes forgotten that the period during which they were in regular use was a comparatively brief one of about fifteen years at most. However, the latter part of that period coincides exactly with the time when most of Purcell's anthems were written.

Tudway should not be interpreted too literally when he writes that 'after the death of King Charles symphonies indeed with instruments were laid aside', for about half of the Purcell anthems that can with reasonable certainty be ascribed to 1687 and 1688 still require strings, but it seems likely that after the accession of William and Mary their use was discontinued. How many strings took part in these performances? On great occasions it is clear that all twenty-four 'violins' were present, but it would be interesting to know how many were considered necessary to balance the reduced strength of the Chapel as it performed at other times. Unfortunately, the published documents refer mainly to the period before Purcell became a Gentleman of the Chapel. In 1671 the usual number was only five, in 1672 six, but this was very likely the number considered sufficient for the performance of symphonies written in only three parts—two violins and bass. In 1678, when eight boys and sixteen men attended at Windsor, the number of strings was twelve, and this seems a more reasonable body for Purcell's four-part writing. What its internal disposition was it is impossible to say with certainty, but on the analogy of some slightly later bands detailed in Carse's *The Orchestra in the XVIIIth Century* we might hazard a guess of 4:4:1:2:1. Perhaps, when a full-scale church organ with sixteen-foot pipes was available, it is possible that the violone or double-bass was dispensed with, and in such cases an extra viola may have been added.

It goes without saying that a modern performance of Purcell's anthems should attempt to reproduce the proportions of the forces to which he himself was accustomed and for which he wrote. For easy reference it may be useful to set these out in tabular form. The total number of Gentlemen can only have been present on such occasions as coronations, so that a minimal figure is given in the suggested break-down into counter-tenors, tenors, and basses:

	Boys	Men	Strings
Full muster:	12	32 (at least 8:8:8)	24 (8:8:3:4:1)
Reduced forces (Windsor, etc.,):	8	18 (at least 4:4:4)	12 (4:4:1:2:1 or 4:4:2:2)

7

An Organist's View of the Organ Works

RALPH DOWNES

The name of Henry Purcell has only to be mentioned in connexion with the organ, and the air is immediately ablaze with echoes of Trumpet Tunes and Voluntaries played on the incomparable Tuba stops for which modern English organ-builders have long been justly renowned, by well-known English organists of our day, using the modern 'arrangements' produced by enterprising publishers in recent years—or alternatively, played with harsher effect possibly, by even better-known French organists, who visit these things on us more or less perennially.

That these compositions exist authentically only in the form of minute trifles for harpsichord or spinet, though a fact well-known to 'specialists' who have taken the trouble to peruse Volume VI of the Purcell Society Edition or the originals themselves, has been overlooked to a remarkable degree by practising musicians both British and foreign, some of whom have so effectively publicized this pseudo-Purcell as to put under total eclipse the true character of the composer's work for the organ and of the instrument for which he composed.

The publication in 1957 of Purcell's organ works, edited by Hugh McLean (Novello), has placed within the reach of all—it would seem—the true picture: and a very excellent

piece of practical scholarship it is. But it is when the practising organist really gets down to the study of these pieces
that he realizes that the creation of a pseudo-Purcell for his
instrument was perhaps justified by a kind of psychological
necessity: for the pieces are disappointing for the most part,
and exhibit few traces of the true and acknowledged genius
of the mature Purcell ('if indeed they are his', as Professor
Westrup drily observes). Even their authenticity is established only at second hand: there is no autograph, and some
of the manuscript copies in which they occur contain
certain other suspect attributions.

It may well be that Purcell's short and busy life as court
composer, singer, and performer, as well as custodian,
tuner, and repairer of all the King's instruments (including
the organs in Westminster Abbey and the Chapels Royal)
left him little time for committing to paper solo organ
compositions which he may largely have improvised as
occasion demanded—there being no other performers to be
supplied with copies in such a case. Such a view is perhaps
supported by the meagre quantity of other keyboard music
which has survived, apart from the small volume of *Lessons
for Harpsichord*, published by his widow.

We can only guess what a wealth of musical enjoyment
was showered on the audience at the famous organ demon-
strations ('The Battle of the Organs') in which he took part
with John Blow, playing on and championing 'Father'
Smith's new instrument at the Temple Church, during his
twenty-sixth year. The organ was a small one by modern
standards, and had no pedals and no 16-foot pitch, but
it was remarkably rich for its time, containing the newly-
imported Continental stops of the Baroque style—mixtures,
reeds such as the Trumpet and Vox Humana, and the
Cornet stop which enjoyed popular favour throughout the

whole of the eighteenth century. Not a trace of this organ remains, and it was heard in original form by no one within living memory. The same melancholy fate has overtaken every one of Smith's instruments, and if one wishes to reconstruct their approximate tonal effect, that can only be realized by visiting one of the few unspoiled organs of the same period in France, Germany, or Holland.

Whatever the explanation of the paucity of surviving compositions, let us now consider what remains: two short Verses and a short piece in C, all stylistically indistinguishable from the work of his contemporaries; a kind of Choral Prelude on the 'Old Hundredth' (attributed equally to Blow), not very original, and interesting mainly as a very early example of registration for the Cornet stop; two longer pieces in D minor, one for Single and one for Double Organ; and a piece in G major.

The works in D minor begin almost alike: it is impossible to establish any chronology, but the piece for Single Organ is stylistically the superior, and is simpler and more direct. The opening consists of a terse fugal exposition, actually in the traditional manner of voluntaries, though charged with the Baroque emotional content found in Christopher Gibbons, Blow, and Matthew Locke. It goes further, however, than any of them: and an added intensity is produced by the dramatic repeated notes, the forceful use of ornamentation, and the effect of *stretto* culminating in a great roulade.

Ex. 3   [Full organ]

(Note: As is frequent at this period, some additional ornamentation is implicit in the text, and must be supplied in

performance: my suggestions for this are shown in brackets.)

Unfortunately, some of the ground thus early and easily won is as quickly lost until the emergence of a new motive:

Ex. 4

which dominates the second half of the piece both rhythmically and melodically leading to a vigorous tonic pedal cadence, the jagged outlines and satisfying harmony of which again seem Purcell's. But some crudity and ungainliness in the intervening harmonic structure suggest an incomplete mastery of the material: some of this has been refined away by Mr. McLean, a doubtful improvement. However, the total impression is undoubtedly one of dramatic grandeur.

The remaining piece in G major is in a different category. Clearly it is descended from the Italian expressive Toccata —those of Frescobaldi were evidently known in England, for two voluntaries attributed to Blow (one of them a 'Double Verse' occurring in the same manuscript collection as this piece) make fairly extensive unacknowledged quotations from two out of his First Book (1614). It is also probable that the Toccatas of Michael Angelo Rossi had already found their way here. The piece under consideration exhibits none of the melodic extravagance or harmonic eccentricity of the Italians' work: and though chromaticism, false relation and the well-worn dissonances of the diminished and augmented triads occur and are even dwelt on, the whole remains tranquil and contemplative, with an air of sweetness and refined comprehensiveness, typically English: this impression is in no-wise contradicted in the neat rounding off of the movement with a sprightly canzona section.

It is a little gem of its kind, within a limited sphere, and that limitation is largely instrumental.

Ex. 5   [Soft]

Conclusion begins:-

Trifling as these works may appear, they stand out in sharp relief against the formalized and sometimes vapid organ music of the succeeding generation. But their fragility is such that literal transposition on to the modern English organ may be fatally damaging: these instruments, for all their useful qualities, are not designed for contrapuntal music, and therefore in performance, subterfuges have to be employed, the success of which will vary enormously according to the circumstances encountered.

Nevertheless, these pieces are all we possess: therefore, at least, they must be treasured with gratitude if regretfully: and the pseudo-Purcell must die.

8

Performing Purcell's Music Today

ROBERT DONINGTON

There could hardly be a composer more sympathetic to the present generation than Purcell. Yet three centuries is a long time to bridge. And Purcell's music was left unused for many generations, so that the traditions in which it was originally performed have been long since forgotten. We have therefore certain difficulties in giving Purcell a completely understanding performance: difficulties which would not arise if his traditions had never been interrupted.

In my experience, these difficulties can best be met by a double approach. In the first place, we can find out as much as possible about how his own contemporaries performed his music; we can do this by examining any evidence which survives in written form. That is where scholarship can make a useful contribution.

In the second place, we must trust our own musicianship to respond, not only to this evidence, but above all to the music itself. Unless we are capable of this response, scholarship cannot help us. There is, indeed, much to be found out which musicianship by itself cannot be expected to recover. But still less can we expect to recover it if we allow our scholarship to override our musicianship. We are in the position of explorers who will not neglect any map, however inadequate, left by their predecessors, but who know that when the real difficulties begin, it is to their own good judgement that they must trust.

The most fundamental difficulty, I believe, is how to give practical expression to what I should describe as the romantic character of Purcell's music. This romantic character shows most obviously in his harmony. The heartrending suspensions, which are really written-out long appoggiaturas, in Dido's famous Lament are romantic harmony in the same sense in which the appoggiatura-based progressions in Wagner's *Tristan* are romantic harmony. But we know now —as the previous generation did not know—that the performing style which is right for Wagner's romanticism is not right for Purcell's.

In some quarters, the reaction has gone too far. We are told that it is out of style to romanticize early music at all, and that we need an unimpassioned rendering to which the term 'objective' (first introduced by Schweitzer in connexion with J. S. Bach) has been applied. But what do Purcell's own contemporaries tell us?

They tell us that the serenity they undoubtedly achieved, like all serenity real enough to be worth having, was achieved not by any illusory exclusion of passion but by a genuine richness of experience. The passion as well as the serenity can be recognized in their music, and it could be recognized in their performances.[1] Here is what the English translator wrote (1709) in a footnote to a passage in Raguenet's *Comparison Between the French and Italian Music* (1702) where the turbulence of Italian violin-playing in agitated movements is being contrasted with its lingering sweetness in tender movements:[2]

I never met with any man that suffered his passions to hurry him

[1] For a sample of the evidence the reader is referred to Appendix B.

[2] The translator was probably J. E. Galliard. The entire pamphlet is reprinted, ed. O. Strunk, in *Musical Quarterly*, XXXII, 3 July 1946, pp. 411ff.

away so much whilst he was playing on the violin as the famous Arcangelo Corelli, whose eyes will sometimes turn red as fire; his countenance will be distorted, his eyeballs roll as in an agony, and he gives in so much to what he is doing that he doth not look like the same man.

If that is the impression (not exactly an objective one) made on his hearers by the classical Corelli himself, it is obviously not impassioned emotion that we have to be afraid of when interpreting a born romantic like Purcell. All we have to be afraid of is reading something into his music which is not there; and this will only happen if we have an insufficiently clear idea of what *is* there. False romanticism is only false because, instead of growing out of the music, it is grafted on to it without due regard for what goes with what: in a word, for style.

But style is not some vague aesthetic mystery. Style is mostly a matter of getting the details reasonably authentic. If we can do that, the genuine romantic feeling which is implicit in Purcell's music will emerge almost of its own accord.

THE PERFORMER'S SHARE IN PROVIDING THE NOTES

We are so accustomed nowadays (with important exceptions in dance music) to having the notes all settled for us by the composer that we find it hard to realize the extent to which the early performers were expected to add to them impromptu as they went along. There is an element of sheer spontaneity about most early music which any good interpretation of it needs to convey, even if there is no actual improvisation going on. Hardly any modern musicians are trained to improve and, indeed, to complete the composition in this impromptu fashion as they go along. The editor has to do it for them in writing. But if the editorial work is well done, and if the performer can keep the necessary freshness of feeling, the result can sound spontaneous without actually being improvised. It is the spirit rather than the fact of improvisation which is important.

When supplying, in writing, many notes which the composer left to be more or less improvised, an editor is providing his performers with a working version which they can use if they have not the skill to provide their own, but can adapt or ignore if they have the necessary skill. There is no final solution; there was never meant to be; there can only be a good solution, by which I mean a good example of the many which are possible.

ACCIDENTALS

Purcell was writing at a time that was only just out of the period in which the performer was expected to regulate his own accidentals, where necessary or desirable, under the loose guidance of the conventions of *musica ficta*.

In this respect, Purcell's *written* parts should normally be performed as they stand, except where there are obvious mistakes or where common sense suggests something not actually written. For example, it was still by no means unusual in Purcell's day to sharpen the seventh degree of the minor scale by writing in the necessary ♯, but to leave it to the performer to sharpen the sixth degree without written indication. In such cases, G♯, F, G♯ is not meant as an augmented second; the F was regarded as so obviously in need of a ♯ that none was written.

The modern rule that the force of an accidental continues until but not beyond the next bar-line was not yet established in Purcell's day. Thus, a passage written as at Ex. 6 is almost certainly intended as at Ex. 7; whereas, on the contrary, a

passage written as at Ex. 8 is quite certainly intended as at
Ex. 9.

Ex. 6

As perhaps written then

Ex. 7

As written now

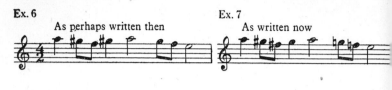

Ex. 8

As perhaps written then

Ex. 9

As written now

In Ex. 6 the composer would further have relied on an
accepted disposition for stepwise passages in the minor
mode to go up sharp but come down flat. If, however, he
wanted to make doubly sure, his notation would probably
have been as at Ex. 10.

Ex. 10

or:

Observe that our ♮ had no place in the standard notation
of seventeenth-century England. Thus ♭ was used to cancel
♯, and ♯ was used to cancel ♭.

So much for the written parts; but there is also the accompaniment and the ornamentation, neither of which
was usually written out. The accidentals which need to be
supplied for an ornamental embellishment are mostly clear
from the prevailing tonality; but those required for the
accompaniment are not always obvious, nor are they always
shown by the figuring. There are still a few remnants of

musica ficta which a figured-bass accompanist in Purcell's music should know.

There is first of all the rule concerning the sharpened leading note. In the case of music as relatively recent as Purcell's, this rule can be put quite simply in Agazzari's[1] brief statement: 'All cadences, whether intermediate or final, need the major third' whether indicated or not. This, however, applies only to important cadences, not to passing cadences. The major third in question is the sharp leading note on the penultimate dominant.

There is next the Picardy third, another old convention. 'In a final cadence the last note must always be taken with a sharp sign', i.e., major, whether so indicated or not.[2] Niedt[3] adds the reservation: 'French composers do the opposite, but not everything is good just because it comes from France.' This reservation is interesting, but possibly too sweeping; moreover, though French influence was strong in Purcell's music, Italian influence was stronger. I feel sure, from practical experience, that the convention of making major the final tonic chord of a minor movement can be applied to Purcell where the result sounds convincing.

ORNAMENTAL EMBELLISHMENT

The embellishment left to the performer by seventeenth and eighteenth-century composers is 'ornamental' only in the sense that it can take any appropriate form without changing the substance of the music; not in the sense that it can be left out entirely. At the astonishingly late date of

---

[1] Agostino Agazzari, *Del suonare sopra il basso* . . . (Sienna, 1607).

[2] Wolfgang Ebner, German transl. in J. A. Herbst, *Arte prattica e poetica* (Frankfurt, 1653).

[3] *Friedrich Erhardt Niedt, Musicalische Handleitung* (Hamburg, 1700), VII, 6.

c. 1805, Dr. Burney could still write in Rees's *Cyclopedia*.[1] that 'an adagio in a song or solo is, generally, little more than an outline left to the performer's abilities to colour. . . . If not highly embellished, [slow notes] soon excite languor and disgust in the hearers.'

There is a famous early eighteenth-century Amsterdam edition of Corelli's violin sonatas, which was afterwards pirated in London, showing the adagios printed in parallel versions: the long, slow notes as ordinarily published (and as nowadays *performed*, with soporific effect); and the cascades of very rapid notes as Corelli himself allegedly performed them. There is a large quantity of similar evidence from the seventeenth and eighteenth centuries, including examples from English sources. A number of English songs of the period are known in the ornamental versions favoured by particular singers, while the art of improvising instrumental variations on a given ground was nowhere carried further than in the examples in Christopher Simpson's *Division Violist* of 1659.

There are instrumental movements by Purcell which, for their full effect, require a continuous light ripple of added ornamentation. But the important word here is *light*. Anything at all heavy, either in the added notes or in their manner of performance, will at once defeat its own object, which is not to add weight to the texture but to enliven it. Whether written out by the composer or left to the performer, this kind of figuration should always sound as if it had only at that very moment been thought of, so that it seems spontaneous even when it is the result of forethought.

In his vocal movements, Purcell usually wrote out his melodic figuration with more completeness than he did in the instrumental movements just mentioned. Such an

[1] s.v. Adagio.

approach to completeness was unusual in a baroque composer. J. S. Bach carried it still further, although even in his music there are passages in which additional melodic figuration needs to be added. In Purcell's music, this need arises somewhat more often, but not so often as in many other baroque composers.

Melodic figuration added, either by the performer more or less impromptu, or by the editor in writing, is one of the two main kinds of embellishment described by the old English word 'graces'. The other kind consists of a large number of small specific ornaments, of which the most important are the appoggiatura and the trill. These ornaments are sometimes optional; but at other times they are, in practice, obligatory. Where the context implies an ornament, the gap in melody and harmony which results from leaving out that ornament is really just a plain mistake, like any other kind of wrong note. This is particularly true of the trills implied by a majority of baroque cadences. In Purcell's day, a performer who habitually left out his cadential trills would have been sent back to school again to learn his notes.

The table of ornaments in Purcell's posthumous *Choice Collection . . . for the Harpsichord*, edited by his widow (London, 1696), and not actually known to have been compiled by Purcell himself, is brief, and like all such tables approximate.[1] (See Facsimiles 1 and 2.)

Appoggiaturas in the seventeenth century are mostly of short to moderate length, whereas those of the eighteenth century tend to be either very short or, more commonly,

[1] A *general* knowledge of the baroque musical contexts which imply ornaments is more important than any of these tables. This is a large subject, for which I may perhaps refer the reader to my articles on Ornamentation and Ornaments in the new *Grove*.

Facsimile 1. Rules for Graces from Purcell's *A Choice Collection of Lessons for the Harpsichord or Spinet*, published by his widow in 1696. (*Reproduced by permission of the Trustees of the British Museum.*)

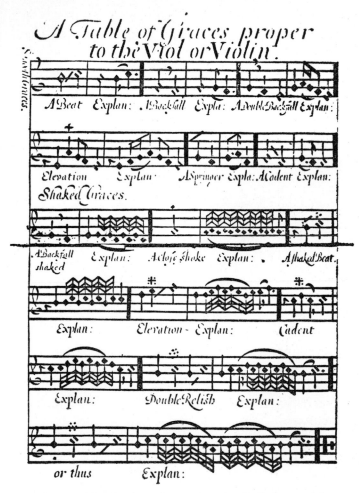

Facsimile 2. Table of Graces from John Playford's *An Introduction to the Skill of Musick*, thirteenth edition, printed for Henry Playford in 1697. (This is the edition for which Purcell had collaborated with Playford.)

very long. Trills, both of the seventeenth and of the eighteenth centuries (with almost negligible exceptions) are begun on their upper notes, and with a good accent on, and often a decided prolongation of, these initial upper notes. Since the upper note is normally a discord, the harmonic effect is at least as important as the melodic.

It is by no means necessary to put in an ornament wherever a sign appears. There were always performers who liked fewer ornaments than others; and so far as the optional ornaments were concerned, this was a matter left to the performer's taste. On the other hand he was always at liberty, within reason, to add ornaments where no signs were written. And he was, of course, obliged to add the full complement of cadential trills, as well as certain appoggiaturas, for which the signs were generally absent just because the need was so obvious.

CONTINUO ACCOMPANIMENTS

Preparing continuo accompaniments more or less impromptu from a figured bass was perhaps the greatest of all the challenges to a performer in connexion with the actual notes of the music. As this is the subject of a separate chapter in this book, the following remarks are in the nature of footnotes.

The figures are essentially there to tell the performer what the written parts are doing; they are not there to restrict his liberty. A 6 or a 7 or even a 9 added to a 5-3 chord, or a 4 or a 5 added to a 6-3 chord, is not a crime, provided it is in the style and is musically convincing.[1]

As to how elaborate an accompaniment should be, that depends partly on the performer's taste (which varied in

[1] cf. F. T. Arnold, *Art of Accompaniment from a Thorough-Bass* (London, 1931), Ch. XXI, § II.

Purcell's time as it does today) and partly on the requirements of the music (which vary still more). It is always
worth remembering the common-sense rule of damping
down the elaboration when the written parts are themselves
in elaborate motion, but opening up when they are not.

THE PERFORMER'S SHARE IN THE EXPRESSION

Apart from the notes, there were, in Purcell's time,
certain conventions influencing the expression—conventions
which are not obvious to unaided musicianship, but which
have to be recovered from contemporary evidence. This
evidence is not always clear enough, or close enough in
time or place, for the matter to be an easy one. But we are
beginning to agree on the main conclusions, and the fact
that we never shall agree on their exact application is
entirely desirable, since such individual differences are, and
always have been, an important part of the value of good
interpretation.

TEMPO AND RUBATO

Tempo is among the responsibilities of the performer. It
is of paramount importance; but it varies in relation to
many other factors in the interpretation, and even in
relation to the acoustics of the building. There is no such
thing as a 'right' tempo in the absolute.

The reader will find in Appendix B what may or may not
be Purcell's own rules connecting tempo with a variety of
time-signatures such as C and ₵; and such rules abound in
the contemporary text-books. They are, however, so
contradictory as to make it obvious that the practice of
composers was quite arbitrary. This was recognized by the
most thoughtful writers from Pierre Maillant in 1610, who
admitted that 'the signs . . . are superfluous and useless . . .

everything is now in confusion', down to the Abbé Laugier in 1754, who pointed out that 'each interprets the time-movement in the light of his own imagination'. In 1650, Kircher, whose account is particularly full and painstaking,[1] wrote of 'this most confused subject (confusissimam materiam)' and 'utter nonsense (tota farrago)' adding that the most experienced composers used C and ₵ 'for one and the same sign (pro unico signo)'. Heinichen, in course of another lengthy exposition, likewise warns us of their indiscriminate use in practice.[2] And indeed we find early editions and manuscripts and even autographs showing different time-signatures in the same passages with remarkable inconsistency. It is, therefore, obviously impossible to rely on time-signatures as a precise indication of tempo. There was, indeed, an imprecise and unreliable understanding that 2 or ₵ should suggest a faster tempo than C, and 2 or 𝇈 than ₵, etc. Those 'faster' signatures often (but very far from always) go with two, rather than four, changes of harmony in the bar (an important point for continuo accompanists); and sometimes a rhythmic pulse of two-in-a-bar can be sensed in the music. But it *is* from the music and not from the time-signatures that the performer has to find his tempo and his pulse.

A change from duple to triple time (shown by 3 or other triple time-signature) may with much greater reliability be taken to indicate an increase of speed, often amounting to $\frac{3}{2}$ ○ = C ♩ or $\frac{3}{4}$ ♩ = C ♩ etc. Even here, the actual amount of the increase is a variable quantity, which, like all other tempo decisions, can only be found by innate musicianship.

Time-words such as grave, adagio, presto, etc. are also

[1] Athanasius Kircher, *Musurgia Universalis* (Rome, 1650), pp. 679, 682, 684.

[2] J. D. Heinichen, *General-Bass* (Dresden, 1728), Part I, Ch. IV, §. 48ff.

unreliable and inconsistent in their connotations, as may be seen in Appendix B. The most valuable recommendation for a modern performer to bear in mind is that he should not take fast movements too fast or slow movements too slow.

In Purcell's trio-sonatas we find movements headed Largo, with the time-signature $\frac{3}{2}$, which become much too sluggish if taken with anything like the slowness of a common-time Largo (itself faster, in Purcell, than Grave or Adagio); they need a good swinging 'tempo di minuetto' to make their natural effect. And, on the other hand, many of the allegros, especially those in canzona form, need a very steady 'allegro moderato' if the rapid changes of harmony in their close counterpoint are to unfold convincingly.

Fluctuations within the main tempo are not ordinarily shown in baroque music, but the evidence tells us that they were intended. Mace,[1] writing in Purcell's lifetime, wanted beginners to learn strict time-keeping first, but added:

When we come to be *Masters*, so that we can *command all manner of Time* at our *own Pleasures*; we then *take Liberty*, (and very often . . .) to *Break Time; sometimes Faster*, and *sometimes Slower*, as we perceive the *Nature of the Thing Requires* . . .

This, of course, includes rallentandos, which we find Frescobaldi describing as early as 1614 in the preface to his *Toccatas* of that year. Baroque music is full of cadences, and it would be intolerably disturbing to the natural momentum of the music if we slowed down for each of them. Nevertheless, the most important ones usually need to be acknowledged by some yielding in the tempo, however slight. Often the barest resilience, scarcely perceptible as a rallentando, is quite enough, and anything more than this will

---

[1] Thomas Mace, *Musick's Monument* (London, 1676), p. 81.

sound cumbersome. Yet to avoid any resilience at all gives the music that machine-like rhythm which does more to destroy its true vitality than most other such misconceptions. We need, in short, a certain musical tact, sensitive above all to the implications of the harmony.

Final cadences naturally incline to slightly more conspicuous rallentandos than intermediate cadences. The habit of charging through a baroque movement with unyielding impetus until the last bar or two, and then suddenly putting on all the brakes as hard as possible, has no justification either in music or in scholarship. A rallentando needs starting early enough to take its own reasonable gradation. However, it is also true that the rallentando must not be exaggerated. A slight rallentando but a shapely one is perhaps the most usual requirement.

RHYTHM: DOTS AND INEQUALITY

Rhythm to a modern performer is a matter governed mainly by the lengths of the written notes; but to a baroque performer it was more a matter of expression, and was governed largely by convention.

In modern music, a dot after a note increases its length by half; not, of course, precisely, but as nearly as ordinary freedom of expression permits.

In baroque notation the dot may have the same effect; but it may also increase the length by any other appropriate amount.

For example, we may often enough meet with a melodic line in which one or more dotted notes occur. If these are an integral part of the melody, in no way standing out from any other part of it, and in no way dominating the rhythm of it, then their value will probably be very much the same as the modern value: i.e. as nearly exact as free

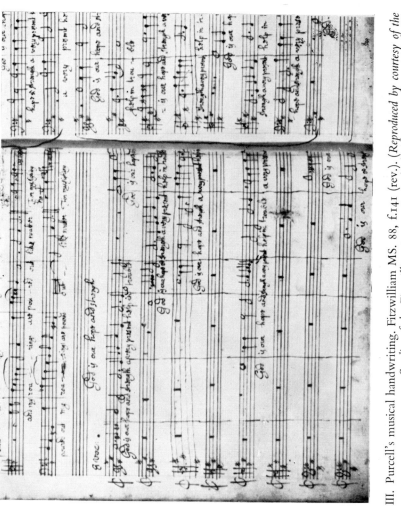

III. Purcell's musical handwriting. Fitzwilliam MS. 88, f.141 (rev.). (Reproduced by courtesy of the Syndics of the Fitzwilliam Museum, Cambridge.)

expression (whether then or now) permits. But if they stand out from the melody, or dominate its rhythm, as independent rhythmic figures in their own right, then a baroque convention applies to them which is no longer currently accepted, though to some extent all good musicians still follow it without realizing that they do so. By this convention, the dot is decidedly lengthened, the note after the dot is correspondingly shortened, and the two are separated by a silence of articulation taken out of the time of this lengthened dot. We generally call this 'double-dotting', though without meaning that the lengthening has to be exactly that. In place of the silence of articulation, the notes may alternatively be slurred, with a more expressive but less brilliant effect.

The following extracts from the Chaconne in Purcell's Trio Sonatas (No. VI of the second set), show examples of dotted notes:

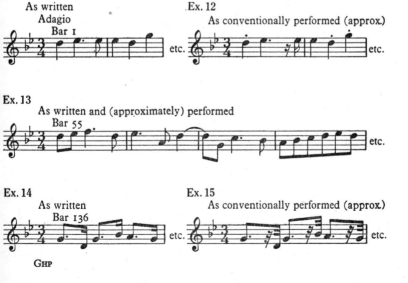

Ex. 11
As written
Adagio
Bar 1
etc.

Ex. 12
As conventionally performed (approx.)
etc.

Ex. 13
As written and (approximately) performed
Bar 55
etc.

Ex. 14
As written
Bar 136
etc.

Ex. 15
As conventionally performed (approx.)
etc.

GHP

There are further extensions of the same principle:

♩♪ may become approximately ♩. ⅋ ♪

♫. may become ♫..

♩. ♫ may become ♩.. ♫

♩. ♬ may become ♩ ⅋ ⅋ ♬

♩ ⅋ ♫ may become ♩⅋⅋♫

♩♫ may stand for ♫♬ or ♩ ⅋ ♫ or ♩⅋⅋♫

⅋ ♫♩ will almost certainly become ⅋ ⅋ ♫♩. ♩ or ⅋⅋⅋♫♩.♫

and so with numerous other possibilities of the same kind.

In compound triple time (whether written as such, or as triplets in common time, &c.), the normal practice in seventeenth- and early eighteenth-century music is as follows:—

♩.♪♪♪ and ♪♪♪♪ may both stand for ♪♪♪.

An example of this occurs in bar 174 of the same Chaconne:

Ex. 16   As written   etc.

Ex. 17   As intended   etc

Individual instances of the performance of dotted notes are often difficult to decide; but a few doubtful decisions either way are of no real importance. What is of importance is the radical improvement in zest and crispness which follows any reasonably enterprising application of the principle itself. Few changes in the direction of greater authenticity have a more enlivening effect.[1]

A further rhythmic convention concerns 'inequality'. By this term is meant the treatment of a series of notes, neither very fast nor very slow, mainly in stepwise motion, and written evenly. They are, however, performed unevenly, 'because', wrote Saint-Lambert in 1702, 'this unevenness makes them more graceful'.[2]

The situation in which the convention of 'inequality' applies were never clearly defined, and they are, once again, often difficult to recognize in practice. The following hints may be helpful.[3]

The notes to which 'inequality' can be applied will be the shortest notes to occur at all numerously in the movement. If these shortest notes are either faster or slower than a moderate speed, 'inequality' becomes ineffectual, and perhaps unpleasant; it should therefore not be applied to them. Again, if the movement has a vigorous or march-like character, 'inequality' can only detract from that character, and should not be applied. Further, although a few leaps occurring in a mainly stepwise progression do not preclude inequality, a melody mainly progressing by leaps

[1] Many excellent suggestions for the true conventional performance of dotted notes in Purcell will be found in the new (not in the old) volumes of the Purcell Society's edition, now under the general editorship of Professor Anthony Lewis.

[2] Michel de Saint-Lambert, *Principes du Clavecin* (Paris, 1702).

[3] I have gone into somewhat more detail in *Grove*, s.v. 'notes inégales'; but the main principles are those given here.

is not of the kind to which 'inequality' was intended to apply.

The convention of 'notes inégales' was most highly cultivated in (but not confined to) France. Performers could give the notes an expressive lilt by somewhat lengthening the first and shortening the second (*lourer*); they could give them piquancy by decidedly shortening the first and lengthening the second (*couler*); if, among the evenly-written notes thus performed unevenly, they came across some notes written dotted, they marked the contrast by very decidedly 'double-dotting' them (*pointer*).

Examples of the *couler* are very commonly found written out in Purcell's vocal parts, as if he particularly favoured this effect and wanted to make sure of getting it.

The *lourer*, however, was always the most typical of the various forms of 'inequality', and there seems little doubt that Purcell got this from his performers in any case. French influence had been paramount in England under Charles II. It remained strong even in Purcell's more Italianate style. And in many of his passages this French lilt is so beautiful that it seems innately as well as historically probable. This probability is always at its strongest where the notes (or enough of them to drop the hint) are written slurred in pairs (as they must anyhow be slurred in perform-ance). If three or more are written slurred together, 'in-equality' is ruled out; and there are various other means of contra-indicating it, none of which, however, occurs as far as I know in Purcell.

The *lourer* and its accompaning *pointer* are both illustrated in the following example from bars 144ff. of Purcell's ode 'Hark, how the wild musicians sing'.[1]

[1] Vol. 27 of the Purcell Society's new edition, ed. Dennis Arundell (but the *lourer* and *pointer* are my suggestion, not his).

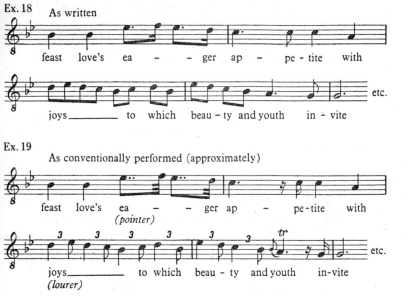

Ex. 18 As written

feast love's ea - - ger ap - pe - tite with

joys_____ to which beau - ty and youth in - vite etc.

Ex. 19 As conventionally performed (approximately)

feast love's ea - - ger ap - pe - tite with
(pointer)

joys_____ to which beau - ty and youth in - vite etc.
(lourer)

PHRASING AND ARTICULATION

The present generation of good musicians has got into
close enough touch with Purcell to grasp his phrase endings
intuitively; but in performance these phrase endings,
though recognized, are seldom made audible enough. This
is not necessarily a matter of holding up the time; it is
usually a matter of taking a short 'silence of phrasing' out of
the time of the last note of the old phrase before beginning
the new. Less frequently, it may be necessary to add a
'comma' to the time.

Within the phrase, we need more 'silences of articulation'. The ability to sustain a smooth cantabile is as necessary
in Purcell as in Bellini; but so is a sense of where to break
the line. The note before a syncopated note, for example,
needs to be shortened by a silence of articulation (as if, in

modern notation, there were a staccato dot over it). And there can be no doubt, on a comparison of many small points of evidence, that the ordinary bread-and-butter manner of stringing together unslurred notes of moderate duration was less smooth and more articulate than our modern training suggests. Attention to this most important detail brings immediate vitality to many quick movements in Purcell which might otherwise move a little stolidly. His romanticism is of a more aerated brand than Wagner's, and needs a lighter texture.

TEXTURE AND DYNAMICS

This lightening of the texture is particularly important when, as so often in Purcell, that texture is of a contrapuntal nature. In the string fantasies, for example, and to some extent in the trio sonatas, each player should take his entry decisively and with that indescribable sense of significance which distinguishes thematic from subordinate matter; then as he hears the next entry coming in, he should get out of the way by lowering both the volume and the intensity of his playing. That was the method recommended in the sixteenth century for polyphonic music, and it is just as valuable in Purcell, or for that matter in Bach. The structure stands out as it is meant to do, no one has to force his entry through a mass of competing sound, and the music makes sense without an effort. The texture itself glitters with ever-changing lights and shades.

The same play of light and shade is needed in the smaller dynamic contrasts and gradations. The theory now fashionable with some reformers under the name of 'terrace-dynamics', to the effect that baroque musicians favoured a long unbroken stretch on one dynamic level followed by another level similarly sustained, is not supported by the evidence. 'We play Loud or Soft, according to our fancy, or the humour of the music . . . some time . . . in one and the same Note' (Simpson, 1659);[1] 'The Viol and Violin excell in lowdning, softning, and continuing a Note or Sound' (Locke, 1672);[2] 'swellings of prodigious length' (Raguenet, 1702);[3] 'courage as well as skill to fill and swell where the harmony required an emphasis' (North,[4] early eighteenth century, but reminiscing of Purcell's lifetime): these are typical phrases, and the last draws attention to a crucial principle. Normal crescendos and diminuendos, louds and softs, are integral to baroque music in so far as they grow out of that music, following rises and falls in the melodic outline and intensifications and relaxations in the harmony. It is only dynamic effects imposed on the music for effect's sake which are harmful. But this is basically a principle of good musicianship in any style.

INSTRUMENTAL STYLE AND TECHNIQUE

Modern wind players generally fall in with the technical requirements of seventeenth or eighteenth-century music very readily, provided they are well coached in the stylistic requirements already discussed. This is not the case, however, with modern string players, whose basic training has evidently diverged much further from the baroque norm. The

[1] Christopher Simpson, *Division Violist* (London, 1659), 2nd ed. (*Division-Viol*) 1667, p. 10 (facsimile ed. Nathalie Dolmetsch, London, 1955).

[2] Matthew Locke, *Observations upon a Late Book*, (London, 1672), p. 36.

[3] François Raguenet, *A Comparison Between the French and Italian Music* (Paris, 1702), Engl. transl. ? J. E. Galliard (London, 1709), ed. O. Strunk, *Musical Quarterly*, XXXII, 3, p. 426.

[4] MS. Autobiography, ed. Jessop, (London, 1890): see the whole passage Sect. 94ff.

modern Tourte-pattern incurved bow is also rather different from the old straight or slightly outcurved bow in its effect on tone-quality and articulation; but this difference, though not by any means negligible, can be minimized with fair success in practice.

The primary difficulty is to articulate an ordinary series of detached notes without too much legato or too much staccato. Our present 'détaché' is not, in fact, detached enough. Our staccato is too detached, and our spiccato too out of the ordinary for a regular effect (though it is perfectly in style and period as a virtuoso effect).

The evidence[1] for the early technique of the violin points to a bowing style well 'into the string' for the body of the note. At the join, the elasticity of the bow is allowed to lighten its pressure almost, but not quite to the extent of leaving the string. This gives more resonance between strokes than the staccato, but more separation than the détaché, and a more relaxed feeling than the spiccato. I have suggested calling it the 'sprung détaché'.

For moderately short notes the best part of the bow is normally about half-way between the point and the middle, with an easy movement of the arm and a relaxed wrist. The flow of notes should, indeed, sound easy and relaxed— neither forced nor sticky; neither disconnected nor merged. The frequent modern practice of taking such notes at the heel and from the air is absolutely unwarranted by the evidence and as harmfully out of style as it could be. The notes sound not less, but more brilliant if they are allowed to ripple along without the least sense of effort.

[1] A selection will be found in my contribution on Violin Playing to the new *Grove*. See also David D. Boyden, 'The Violin and Its Technique in the Eighteenth Century', *Musical Quarterly*, Jan. 1950, p. 18.

The next consideration is the quality of tone. It is remarkable how many early descriptions of good string tone (e.g. Playford, Simpson, and Mace from late seventeenth-century England alone) include the adjective 'clear'. Leopold Mozart in the mid-eighteenth century wanted 'an honest and virile tone from the violin'; and it is a suggestive description. Almost any kind of violin tone, including that produced in high positions and by every variety of bow speed and pressure, has *some* place in early violin playing; the virtuoso violinists were exploring most available possibilities soon after Purcell's death, if not before. But for average workaday purposes, and certainly for the greater part of Purcell's string writing, the tone wanted is indeed clear and transparent, honest and virile. That means using mainly the lower positions; and above all it means using mainly a steady speed of bow stroke with a fair pressure into the string. Too much bow—i.e. too fast and too light on the string—is one of the chief mistakes detracting from the natural brilliance and crisp sparkle proper to early string writing.

Accentuation should also be crisp rather than massive, and more often achieved by an instantly released finger-pressure on the bow than by heavy arm-pressure or by taking the attack from the air. A silence of articulation *before* this crisp pressure will greatly increase the effect of accentuation.

Vibrato is entirely legitimate, there being a number of seventeenth-century references to its use and techniques. Some authors preferred to treat it as an ornament for rather sparing use only; but others regarded it as an enlivenment of the normal tone. In the 1730s, Geminiani[1] unreservedly

[1] F. Geminiani, *Art of Playing on the Violin* (London, 1740, p. 8, facsimile, ed. David D. Boyden, Oxford, 1952).

recommended it as making the 'Sound more agreeable, and for this Reason it should be made use of as often as possible'. But a very massive vibrato does undoubtedly sound anachronistic, just as an opulent quality of tone sounds anachronistic. Early music should seldom sound massive in any way.

And that, perhaps, best sums up the difference. The Wagnerian style has weight and power; its climaxes achieve a wonderful intensity. The style of Purcell is sharper and depends more on impetus. This does not make it any the less intense. But its intensity has to be built up in a more concentrated way.

PURCELL'S DANCES

By Imogen Holst

Playford's *English Dancing Master, or Plaine and easie Rules for the Dancing of Country Dances*, is one of the few surviving sources of English dance notation in the late seventeenth century. The ninth edition, published in 1695, contains the tune of the hornpipe in the first act of *Dioclesian*. It is re-named *The Siege of Limerick* and is given with full instructions as to how it is to be danced. The steps and figures are not the same as those that would have been danced in stage performances of *Dioclesian*, for the Playford country dances were mostly 'longways for as many as will', and were meant for social enjoyment, not for spectacular entertainment. But the 'plaine and easie Rules' do, at any rate, give us some of the ways in which Purcell's music was actually danced during the last year of his life. And, as such, they can be helpful in phrasing his instrumental music, for the steps fit the tunes as inevitably as the words fit the songs.

Today, when dancing a seventeenth-century country dance, one of the first and most obvious things that one

learns about the music is that all the repeats are essential.
Without them, the dancers would be stranded on the wrong
side of the set, with no hope of getting back to their own
partners. The convention of playing an instrumental
repetition *piano* or *pianissimo* may have its uses in the concert
hall, but it is seldom helpful to the dancers, who find infinite
variety in going through the same pattern of movements
with each new couple they meet.

At every double-bar, the dancers make a very slight
obeisance to their partners or 'contrary' partners. This courtesy movement, which is scarcely more than a nod of recog-
nition, needs no extra time to perform; it is only at the
very end of the dance that partners 'honour' each other with
a full-length bow and curtsy, to a rallentando in the music.
The least hint of a calculated slowing down at any other
cadence can have a disastrous effect, for the dancer uses the
courtesy movement, with its slight give at the knees, as a
kind of springboard for the lift that will carry him into the
new phrase. If the player digs himself in at the cadence, the
unfortunate dancer is unable to adjust his balance: he
suffers a physical shock that is just as uncomfortable as the
sensation, when going downstairs, of landing on a last step
that isn't there.

This wrong phrasing can be particularly frustrating in the
cadences of a Purcell hornpipe, such as the following
example from *Abdelazar*, which, in the early eighteenth
century, was danced as 'The Hole in the Wall':

Ex. 20

Even sensitive string-players have been known to arrive

on this last note with an unwanted stress that interrupts the flow of the music and wrecks the dancers' hopes of an instinctively-phrased repeat. One of the easiest ways for a non-dancer to realize what is wanted is to look at the song 'There's not a swain', where the words take care of the phrasing and dynamics:

Ex. 21

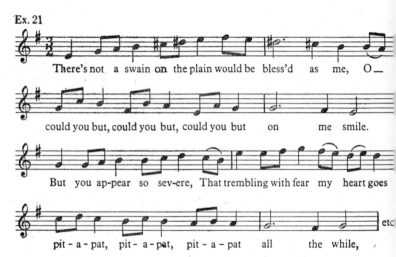

There's not a swain on the plain would be bless'd as me, O—

could you but, could you but, could you but on me smile.

But you ap-pear so sev-ere, That trembling with fear my heart goes

pit - a - pat, pit - a - pat, pit - a - pat all the while, etc

It is a perfect hornpipe: so perfect that it is almost impossible to sit still through it while hearing it sung. At the cadences, the dancers' courtesy movement—as in other hornpipes—is already implied in the harmonies: the six-four chord needs to be given its suitable weight before it can relax at the third-beat resolution. When a Purcell dance tune is phrased as unerringly as if it were a song, the dancer can respond to any rubato the player may wish to make, and, if he is sure of his musician, he himself can make an unrehearsed rubato in his dancing, knowing that the player will accompany him just as if he were a singer.

There are other lessons to be learnt from dancing Purcell's

hornpipes. One of the most important is that the tempo must not be too fast. With one step to each beat, the dancer may have only six beats in which to cast off, (that is, turn away from his partner) to go down the set to the second place, to join hands with his neighbour, and to come up again to his original place. In order to cover the distance in six steps, the dancer will need to make a wide sweep in the figure; when casting off, he will probably lean over at an angle to help himself round the corner, and his steps will have to have the weight of his whole body behind them if they are to carry him back to his place by the end of the second bar. If the tune is played too fast, he will be compelled to cut his corner too close, with the result that his energy will fritter away in little upright, mincing steps.

Another fault to be avoided in playing hornpipes is the habit of marking the syncopated notes with unnecessary accents. Seventeenth-century musicians called their syncopation 'driving'.[1] The dancer relies on the impetus of the driving to carry him along; accents on the syncopated notes create pitfalls of static silence that trip him up on his journey. If there are to be any stresses on the syncopated notes, they must be flexible stresses within a long, continuous line of melody.

Some instrumentalists, in their misguided efforts to be helpful to the dancers, are inclined to destroy the long line of a tune by deliberately making all their staccato notes too prickly. But country dancing, however buoyant and airy it may be, is essentially a legato occupation. There are, of course, frequently recurring moments when, for the

[1] 'Syncope, or Driving a Note, is, when after some shorter Note which begins the Measure or Half-measure, there immediately follow two, three, or more Notes of a greater quantity, before you meet with another short Note (like that which began the driving.)' Christopher Simpson, *Compendium*, 1665.

fraction of a second, the dancer's two feet are both in the air. But this does not mean that he consciously goes through the motions of picking his feet up. Only beginners do that, and they so soon get exhausted that they either give up altogether or else acquire enough technique to carry their own weight effortlessly over the ground. The instrumentalist's staccato notes in a Purcell dance need to be as casual and light-hearted as the singer's consonants in the 'pit-a-pat' of 'There's not a swain'. When this happens, there can be no danger of the dancers wearing themselves out unnecessarily; they will be able to move, with the freedom of confidence, to the music that has been described as 'the easiest in the world to dance to'.

9

Purcell's Handwriting

FRANKLIN B. ZIMMERMAN

The accuracy and the completeness of a list of any composer's autographs both depend upon the certainty with which his handwriting can be identified. Purcell's hand[1] is one of those which are almost always immediately recognizable. For this reason it has not been necessary to fall back upon the analytical methods of the calligrapher or the papyrologist in identifying the autographs listed in Appendix A. The 'personality' revealed in Purcell's handwriting—if I may go so far without venturing into the necromantic realm of graphology[2]—makes so strong an impression upon the observer that once seen it is not likely to be forgotten. For this reason, subsequent identifications scarcely seem to require comparison with known authentic autographs.

Nevertheless, there are a great many Purcell autographs now missing which may one day be discovered. There are also a great many manuscripts labelled 'Purcell's autograph' which are not in his hand. For these two reasons, there is some purpose in outlining here a few of the characteristic features of Purcell's handwriting.

The robust style of his literal hand—best described,

[1] The only previous study on Purcell's autographs is A. Hughes-Hughes, 'Henry Purcell's Handwriting', *Musical Times*, 1896, pp. 81-3.

[2] For one such venture cf. F. H. Walker, 'Purcell's Handwriting', *Monthly Musical Record*, LXXII, 1942, pp. 155-7.

perhaps, as a 'deliberate scrawl'—is quite unmistakable. The hand is perpendicular, though not rigidly or painstakingly so, and each letter is 'full-blown' and boldly formed. Even though there is something schoolboyish in the overall appearance of the writing this is plainly the hand of a man who thought clearly and methodically and knew what he was about. In this connexion it is worth noting that errors indicating lapses of concentration and miscalculations of available space are quite rare in Purcell's autograph copies— even in those apparently done in a hurry.

Purcell's musical hand, though equally characteristic, was more easily simulated by followers and admirers. This may explain why a number of manuscripts in the hands of other men have been attributed to Purcell at one time or another (see Section III of Appendix A). For this reason, it may be well to single out here a few of the most characteristic features of his musical as well as of his literal hand.

Of the capital letters Purcell used, the following seem to be the most characteristic: A, C, E, H, I, L, M, O, P, S, T, and Y. The forms of these letters as they most commonly occur in Purcell's autographs may be seen in the plates reproduced with this essay. Among lower-case letters the same may be said of Purcell's d (nearly always with a very large loop), e (of which there are two forms, the modern e and the old backwards ɘ), f, h, s, t, y, and z. Other signs important for purposes of identification include the ampersand (&) and the contractions 'ye' and 'yt'. Again, most of these may be seen in the plates.

The most easily recognizable musical signs which Purcell used include the clefs, key-signatures, and time-signatures. Of these the clefs are perhaps the most distinctive. The G-clef (as shown in the Monteverdi transcript) is quite Purcellian and typical of his usage in both early and late manuscripts. The C-clefs shown on this same plate are even more characteristic. Incidentally, these are a rather early form of the Purcellian C-clef, which evolved from this sign: ▤ in the very early autographs to this: ▤ in the later ones. The transitional state of these clefs is particularly clear in Plate III, where both types occur side by side. The F-clef underwent a similar evolution from ▤ to ▤. Both forms are to be found in Plate III. Other important Purcellian signs include the pause signs and the 'end of composition' signs.

I cannot end without mentioning one of the most distinctive features of Purcell's handwriting: the exact placing of all notational symbols. These symbols are so placed that scarcely ever is there any room for doubt as to their meaning, even in the Gresham Manuscript or in some of the later works in the Royal Music autograph, which betray signs of considerable haste. Even the large, sprawling minims and semibreves (like those shown in the Monteverdi transcript) may be seen to have been carefully placed, so that the reader or performer cannot have the slightest doubt as to Purcell's intentions. This feature has more than once served to disprove a supposed autograph, which might otherwise have been considered just possibly genuine.

Appendix A

PURCELL'S AUTOGRAPHS[1]

NIGEL FORTUNE and FRANKLIN B. ZIMMERMAN

Introduction

I Works by Purcell in his autograph
II Works not by Purcell but in his hand
III Supposititious autographs
IV Reliable non-autograph manuscript sources of major works by Purcell

ABBREVIATIONS

Barber	Music Library, Barber Institute of Fine Arts, University of Birmingham
B.M.	British Museum, London
Bodleian	Bodleian Library, Oxford
Fitzwilliam	Fitzwilliam Museum, Cambridge
Royal Academy	Royal Academy of Music, London
Sibley	Sibley Library, Eastman School of Music, Rochester, N.Y.
Stanford	Memorial Library of Music, Stanford University, California.
Tenbury	St. Michael's College, Tenbury, Worcs.

INTRODUCTION

Section I of the following catalogue is basically a list of works by Purcell surviving in his autograph. First, the contents of the four volumes preserved in the Fitzwilliam Museum, Cambridge, and the British Museum and Gresham College, London, and consisting to a great extent of Purcell's music in his own hand, are listed as they occur. Works not by Purcell copied by him and works by Purcell copied by amanuenses

[1] We gratefully acknowledge the assistance given by Mr. Watkins Shaw, Miss M. C. Crum of the Bodleian Library, Oxford, Miss Pamela J. Willetts of the British Museum, the Librarians of the Fitzwilliam Museum, Cambridge, and of the Royal Academy of Music, London, and the Gresham Committee, in the preparation of this appendix.

presumably closely connected with him are included here in order that the reader may obtain a complete view of these important volumes. This section ends with a list, arranged alphabetically by titles, of all other autograph copies of Purcell's works, which are to be found in single manuscripts or in single gatherings within composite manuscripts.

Section II is a list of isolated copies of works by other composers which are to be found in Purcell's hand in composite manuscripts.

Section III is a list of sources that have in the past been thought to be autographs of Purcell. This list would have been very long had we not decided to mention only those manuscripts which have been 'established' as autographs in various catalogues and other published sources and to ignore those which appear to have been labelled 'autograph' for other than scholarly reasons.

To complement these lists Section IV indicates reliable manuscript sources of major works by Purcell for which there are no known autographs. To keep this list from swelling beyond reasonable limits the only works considered are *Dido and Aeneas* and other (so-called) operas, the *Morning and Evening Service* in B flat, the *Te Deum and Jubilate*, and the two sets of trio-sonatas.

In all these lists the titles of vocal works are given in modern spelling. Headings written by Purcell himself to indicate a date or the genre to which a particular work belongs or other important information are reproduced within quotation marks exactly as he wrote them, except that the abbreviations 'ye' and 'yt' and one or two other contractions are written out in full and one or two other trifling adjustments have been made on grounds of practicability. Where Purcell does not state the genre we have added it after the title to correspond with the usual modern terminology.

I. WORKS BY PURCELL IN HIS AUTOGRAPH

There survive three large folio volumes in which Purcell made what appear to be fair copies of his own and other composers' works, arranged by categories. It is the contents of these volumes that take pride of place in the following catalogue. The first (Fitzwilliam MS.88) is dated 1677 (?) to 1682; the second (B.M. Add. MS. 30930) appears to have been begun about 1680 and continued for about three years; and the third (B.M. Royal Music MS.20.h.8) runs from about 1681 to 1690. The paper is the same in all three, and each page contains sixteen staves.

(i) FITZWILLIAM MUSEUM, CAMBRIDGE. MS. 88(23 H 13)

The first of the three volumes of fair copies (measuring 44 × 28 cm.) is devoted to anthems. Most of them are by other composers, flourishing either before or during Purcell's time. This is therefore an important source of music that may be expected to have influenced the composer in his formative years.

There is at either end of the volume an index in Purcell's hand. The date at the head of the front index has for long been a source of dispute: it has been stated, categorically, to be 1673 and 1681 and, tentatively, to be 1687[1] (a date that cannot be taken seriously). It is a very difficult date to decipher, and it is only after an exhaustive scrutiny that we are for the first time prepared to advance it here as our opinion that the true reading is '1677'. This reading accords, moreover, with the fact that on ff. 9v and 14v Blow is styled 'Mr' and on f. 28v 'Dr': Blow received his doctorate on 10 December 1677.

Hughes-Hughes says[2] that the forty-two leaves containing the anthems at the front end of the volume are not in Purcell's hand. We can see why he was led to say this, but would say ourselves that only the first thirty leaves might be called in question and that anyway the assertion requires substantiation. Certainly if these leaves are not in Purcell's hand then many others in the manuscript that are extremely similar to them must also be thrown open to doubt. It is our belief that these leaves (like the rest of the volume) are in Purcell's hand; that they were written in his late 'teens when his handwriting was in a transitional state; and that they are almost certainly his earliest surviving autographs.

Front end On a fly-leaf: 'A Table of all the anthems contain'd in this book Sep: the 13th Anno Domini 1677'

Folios		Titles	Subheadings, original subheadings, and compilers' notes
1	*By Humfrey*	O praise the Lord	Verse anthem
4	„	O Lord, my God	„ „
7	„	Like as the hart	„ „

[1] cf. G. E. P. Arkwright, 'Purcell's church music' (*Musical Antiquary*, I, 1909-10, pp. 241 and 243); idem. in the Purcell Society edition, vol. XIIIa: *Sacred Music*, I (London, 1921), pp. ii-iii; A. Hughes-Hughes, 'Henry Purcell's Handwriting' (*Musical Times*, 1896, p. 82); and J. A. Fuller-Maitland and A. H. Mann, *Catalogue of the Music in the Fitzwilliam Museum, Cambridge* (London, 1893), p. 37.

[2] loc. cit.

Folios		Titles	Subheadings, original subheadings, and compilers' notes
9v	*By Blow*	O sing unto the Lord	Verse Anthem
14v	„	Sing we merrily	„ „
21	*By Humfrey*	Lord, teach us to number	„ „
23v	„	Lift up your heads	„ „
26v	*Anon.*	Unidentified instrumental movement in E minor, in four parts	
28v	*By Blow*	Cry aloud	„ „
31	*By Locke*	Sing unto the Lord	„ „
36v	„	When the Son of man	„ „
38v	„	The Lord hear thee	„ „
40v	„	I will hear what the Lord will say	„ „

Reverse end On a fly-leaf: 'God bless M^r. Henry Purcell/1682 September the 10th'

142v	*By Blow*	O Lord, I have sinned	Verse anthem
141	„	God is our hope	Full anthem with verse
138	„	O God, wherefore art thou?	„ „ „ „
136	*By O. Gibbons*	Hosanna to the Son of David	Full anthem
134v	*By Blow*	Save me, O God	Verse anthem
133v	*By Locke*	Lord, let me know mine end	„ „
131	„	Turn thy face from my sins	Full anthem with verse
129	*By Byrd*	Bow thine ear, O Lord	Full anthem
127v	*By Tallis*	I call and cry	„ „
126	*By Byrd*	Prevent us, O Lord	„ „
125	„	O Lord, make thy servant	„ „
124	*By O. Gibbons*	Lift up your heads	„ „
122v	*By W. Mundy*	O Lord, I bow the knee	„ „
120v	*By T. Tomkins*	O Lord, I have loved	„ „
119v	*By N. Giles*	O give thanks	„ „
118	*By Batten*	Hear my prayer, O God	„ „
116	*By Purcell*	Save me, O God	„ „
114v	*By Child*	Sing we merrily	„ „
112	[*By O. Gibbons*]	Almighty and everlasting God	Full anthem (anonymous here); only the first few bars copied, with space to continue
111	*By Purcell*	Blessed is he whose unrighteousness is forgiven	Verse anthem
108	*By Blow*	My God, my soul is vex'd	„ „
106v	*By Purcell*	Hear me, O Lord, and that soon (second version)	„ „
104	„	Bow down thine ear	
102	„	Man that is born	Funeral sentences
100	„	Remember not, O Lord	Full anthem
99	*By Blow*	O Lord God of my salvation	Verse anthem
96	*By Purcell*	O God, thou hast cast us out	Full anthem, with verse
93v	*By Blow*	Christ being risen from the dead	Verse anthem

Folios		Titles	Subheadings, original subheadings, and compilers' notes
92	*By Purcell*	O Lord God of hosts	Full anthem with verse
89	„	O God, thou art my God	„ „ „ „
			Unfinished, with space to continue
87v	„	Lord, how long wilt thou be angry?	Full anthem with verse
86	„	O Lord, thou art my God	Verse anthem
83v	„	Hear my prayer, O Lord	Full anthem. Unfinished, with space to continue (no complete copy known)

(II) BRITISH MUSEUM. ADD. MS. 30930

The second of the three big books of fair copies (measuring 40·7 × 24·8 cm.) accommodates two types of music. The front of the book is devoted mainly to three- and four-part hymns with continuo, which are settings of metrical versions of the psalms. At the back is instrumental music. With the exception of a few random notes in the middle of f.44 (which is otherwise blank), the whole of this volume is in Purcell's hand.

Some autographs must have been removed at an early date and may have been replaced by blank leaves:[1] in fact, on f.37v Joseph Warren, a nineteenth-century owner of the volume, wrote: '10 leaves have been abstracted here, including the whole of the 4th. 5th. 6th. 7th. 8th. Sonatas. The above is the 9th.' (He later crossed out '7th. 8th.'.) At all events the volume contains many blank leaves, which are of exactly the same sort of paper as those that are written on; while a number of these leaves appear between separate items of music others actually occur during the course of compositions that Purcell must be assumed to have copied on successive leaves. It is probable that this eccentric sequence of leaves originated accidentally when the volume was rebound early in 1896: certainly when Warren described this volume[2] he mentioned blank leaves only between and not during the course of works, and, moreover, his statement that Purcell's remark on f.51v is 'followed by 9 blank pages' is no longer true (there are seven including f.51v itself).

Front end Title on one of the fly-leaves: 'The Works/of Hen; Purcell./Anno Dom. 1680'

Folios	Titles		Subheadings, original subheadings, and compilers' notes
3	Plung'd in the confines of despair	Hymn	
4	O all ye people	„	
6	When on my sickbed	„	

[1] For an amplification of these theories cf. Denis Stevens, 'Purcell's art of fantasia' (*Music and Letters*, XXXIII, 1952, pp. 341-2).

[2] cf. W. Boyce, *Cathedral Music*, ed. J. Warren (London, 1849), vol. II, pp. 18-19.

Folios	*Titles*	*Subheadings, original subheadings, and compilers' notes*
7v	Gloria Patri in C minor	Canon
8v	Jehovah, quam multi	Motet[1]
11	Beati omnes qui timent	,,
13	Domine, non est exaltatum	Motet. Only the first few bars copied, with space to continue (no other copy known)
14	Lord, not to us	Hymn. Unfinished, with space to continue (no complete copy known)
15v	Ah! few and full of sorrows	Hymn. Unfinished, with space to continue. Probably only one section is lacking (no complete copy known)
18	O Lord our governor	Hymn
20v	O, I'm sick of life	,,
22	Lord, I can suffer	,,
23v	Hear me, O Lord, and that soon (first version)	Anthem. Unfinished. Only the first section copied, with little space to continue (no complete copy of this version known, though it is scarcely different from the second in Fitzwilliam MS. 88)
24v	Since God so tender a regard	Hymn
26	Early, O Lord, my fainting soul	,,
28	Hear me, O Lord, the great support	,,

Reverse end

71	No. 1	'Here beginneth the 3 part Fantazia's'
70v	No. 2	Very slightly unfinished, with space to continue (no complete copy known)
69v	No. 3	
68	No. 1	'Here beginneth the 4 part Fantazia's'
67	'Fantazia'	'June the 10. 1680.' The titles are always at the top and the dates between the top two staves
66	'Fantazia'	'June the 11. 1680.'
65	'Fantazia'	'June the 14. 1680.'
64	'Fantazia'	'June the 19. 1680'
63	'Fantazia'	'June the 22. 1680.'
62	'Fantazia'	'June the 23: 80.'
61	'Fantazia'	'June the 30. 80:'
60	'Fantazia'	'August the 18 80.' The day of the month is not certain: it was altered from both '16' and '19'
59	'Fantazia'	'August the 31: 1680.'
58	'Fantazia'	'Feb. the 24th. 1682/3.' Unfinished. Only the first 2½ lines copied, with space to continue (no complete copy known). This looks more like the beginning of a sonata than of a fantasia

[1] Purcell did not himself use the term 'motet'; we use it here to distinguish Latin settings from English.

Folios	Titles	Subheadings, original subheadings, and compilers' notes
57	'Pavan'	
56	'Chacony'	
54	'Overture'	
53	Two short dances in G	Incomplete. First violin and bass only
52v	Another short dance in G	Incomplete. First violin and bass only, on the bottom half of the page. At the end: 'Finis'. These last three pieces no doubt form part of a suite, of which the overture was probably intended as the first movement
51v	No. 1	'Here Begineth the 5 Part: Fantazias'
50	'Fantazia upon one Note'	'Fantazias of 5 Parts'
48	'In nomine' (in 6 parts)	'Here Begineth the 6, 7, & 8 part Fantazia's'
46	'In nomine'	'7 Parts'
43v	No. 1 in B minor	'Sonnata's.' These are from the *10 Sonatas of IV parts*, for two violins, bass and continuo (London, 1697)
41v	'Sonnata' No. 2 in E flat	
39v	'Sonnata' No. 3 in A minor	This sonata, which lacks most of the continuo, ends on a small piece of a leaf numbered 37*, bound in at the top of the volume. On the reverse is part of the Sonata No. 4 in D minor, in Purcell's hand, not copied on to fit but already there before cutting. *See* note to f.32 below
37v	'Sonnata' No. 9 in F	On f.36v three bars have been pasted over the original
35v	'Sonnata' No. 7 in C	
34	'Sonnata' No. 8 in G minor	Lacking most of the continuo part
32	'Sonnata' No. 4 in D minor	Only the first three bars of the violin parts copied, with space to continue. *See* note to f.39v above
31	'Sonnata' No. 10 in D	

(III) BRITISH MUSEUM. ROYAL MUSIC MS. 20.H.8

This is much the fullest of the three volumes of fair copies; it measures 40·4 × 25·2 cm. It contains, at the front, verse anthems (all, except the one by Blow, with strings) and, at the back, welcome songs, odes, songs, duets and secular cantatas.[1]

Purcell indexed only the anthems. His index includes two associated with the last days of King Charles II, 'I will give thanks unto the Lord' and

[1] We use the now accepted term 'cantata' for its convenience and to avoid confusion, although we are well aware that Purcell himself did not use it and that the works in question are not really comparable with contemporary cantatas.

'O Lord, grant the King a long life', which he did not copy, presumably because he was too busy composing the next anthem in this book, 'My heart is inditing', for the coronation of King James II; he did not list this and the three succeeding anthems in his index. (*See* Plate IV.)

These last three anthems, much of the third anthem, and the last three works at the reverse end of the volume are in the hand of an amanuensis, who was possibly Purcell's brother Daniel. The greater part of the previous item at the reverse end is in a third hand. At one or two other places the hand alters slightly but not enough to suggest that it is not still Purcell's. Purcell numbered the works at the reverse end, and he also added subsidiary numbers, which apparently refer to the number of sections making up a work. He also marked certain works at either end with a cross, of the precise significance of which we cannot be sure.

CONTENTS

Front end   Title on one of the fly-leaves:
'A SCORE Booke/Containing Severall Anthems wth Symphonies'

Folios	Titles	Subheadings, original subheadings, and compilers' notes
4	It is a good thing to give thanks	'Anthems'
7v	O praise God in his holiness	
13v	Awake, put on thy strength	Very largely non-autograph.[1] Lacking final chorus
16v	*By Blow:* O pray for the peace	
17v	In thee, O Lord, do I put my trust	
22v	The Lord is my light	
25v	I was glad when they said	
28v	My heart is fixed	
32v	Praise the Lord, O my soul, and all that is within me	
37v	Rejoice in the Lord alway	Lacking inner parts of symphonies
39v	Why do the heathen?	
43	Unto thee will I cry	
48	I will give thanks unto thee, O Lord	A few bars lacking
52 ||	They that go down to the sea in ships	Only a few bars copied; this was abandoned, no doubt, for the same reason that the next two anthems in the index were not copied at all:[1] space was left for all the missing music
53v	My heart is inditing	'one of the Anthems Sung at the Coronation of King James the 2d.'
67	O sing unto the Lord	Not autograph[1]
75	Praise the Lord, O Jerusalem	Not autograph[1]
81	Praise the Lord, O my soul, O Lord my God	Not autograph.[1] Lacking the last few bars

[1] *See* introductory paragraph to this manuscript.

Reverse end Title on one of the fly-leaves (in the hand of Edward Purcell, father of the Edward Purcell who wrote on the fly-leaf at the front end: 'E^d H. Purcell/Grandson to the Author of this Book'): 'Score Booke/Anthems and Welcome songs and other songs all by my father.'

Folios	Titles	Subheadings, original subheadings, and compilers' notes
245v	Swifter, Isis, swifter flow	'A Welcome Song in the Year 1681 For the King'
238	What shall be done in behalf of the man?	'A Welcome Song for his Royall Highness at his return from Scotland in the Yeare 1682'
232v	The summer's absence unconcerned we bear	'A Welcome Song for his Majesty at his return from New Market October the 21—1682'
226	How pleasant is this flowery plain	Cantata
224	We reap all the pleasures	Cantata. Unfinished.
222v	Hark how the wild musicians sing	Cantata
218	Hark, Damon, hark	Cantata
217	Above the tumults of a busy state	Duet
216	While you for me alone had charms	'(The 9th Ode of Horrace imitated) (A Dialouge betwixt the Poet & Lydia)'
215	Haste, gentle Charon	'(A dialouge between Charon & Orpheus.)'
213v	Underneath this myrtle shade	'(The Epicure)'. Duet
212v	No, to what purpose should I speak?	'(The Concealment)'. Song
211v	Draw near, you lovers	Song
211	Let the night perish	'(Jobs Curse)'. Sacred song
210	Amidst the shades and cool refreshing streams	'(Song)'
209	See where she sits	Cantata
207	From hardy climes	'(A Song that was perform'd to Prince George upon his Marriage wth the Lady Ann.)'
201	In a deep vision's intellectual scene	'(M^r. Cowley's complaint)'. Cantata. On f.199 two staves have been pasted over the original
198v	With sick and famish'd eyes	'(Song) out of Mr. Herbert.' Sacred song
197v	Fly, bold rebellion	'The Welcome Song perform'd to his Majesty in the Year 1683'
190	Laudate Cecilliam	'A Latine Song made upon St Cecilia, whoes day is commerated yearly by all Musitians made in the year 1683'. Ode
188	Oh! what a scene	Cantata
186v	Though my mistress be fair	'a 2 voc.'
185v	Soft notes and gently raised	'(A Serandeing Song)'. Cantata.
184v	Silvia, thou brighter eye of night	'(A Seranading Song)'. Duet

Folios	Titles	Subheadings, original subheadings, and compilers' notes
183v	Go, tell Aminta, gentle swain	'2 voc.'
182v	From those serene and rapturous joys	'The Welcome Song perform'd to his Majesty in the year 1684'
175	Cease, anxious world	'(Song On a Ground)'
174v	They say you're angry	'The Rich Rivall out of Mr Cowly'. Song
173	When Teucer from his father fled	Duet
172	If prayers and tears	'(Sighs for our Late Sov'raign King Charles the 2^d)'. Song
170v	[I came, I saw, and was undone]	'(The Thraldome out of Mr Cowley)'. Not copied, but space left for it
169v	In some kind dream	Duet
169	Awake, and with attention hear	'(The 34 chapter of Isaiah paraphras'd by Mr Cowley)'. Sacred song
166	Why are all the Muses mute?	'Welcome Song 1685 being the first Song performd to King James the 2^d.'
157	Here's to thee, Dick	'The Words by Mr Cowley'. Duet
155	Ye tuneful Muses	'Welcome Song 1686'
144v	If ever I more riches did desire	Cantata
140	This poet sings the Trojan wars	'(Anacreon's Defeat)'. Song
139	Sound the trumpet	'Welcome Song 1687'
128	Begin the song	'The Resurrection; out of Cowley's Pindaricks'. Sacred song. Only a very few notes of the beginning copied, with space left to continue
127	*By Carissimi:* Crucior in hac flamma	Duet (anonymous here)
125v	Celestial music	'A Song that was perform'd at Mr Maidwells a school master on the 5th of August 1689 The words by one of his scholars'. Ode. The greater part is non-autograph[1]
116v	Now does the glorious day appear	Ode for Queen Mary's birthday, 1689. Not autograph[1]
105v	Of old when heroes thought it base	Ode (Yorkshire Feast Song). Not autograph[1]
90	Arise my Muse	Ode for Queen Mary's birthday, 1690. Not autograph.[1] Unfinished

(IV) GRESHAM COLLEGE, LONDON. MS.VI.5.6[2]

This autograph volume consists of songs, duets and dialogues, most of them from operas or plays. It is not a companion to the preceding three volumes: it is smaller (21·2 × 28 cm.), and it dates from the end of Purcell's life—all the music in it that can be dated (and that means the greater

---

[1] *See* introductory paragraph to this manuscript.
[2] cf. W. Barclay Squire, 'An unknown autograph of Henry Purcell (*Musical Antiquary*, III, 1911-12, pp. 5-17).

part) was composed between 1690 and 1695. Purcell may have intended it for his own use as a singer or for that of a pupil.

Folios	Titles	Sources, subheadings and notes
1	Now the maids and the men are making of hay	*The Fairy Queen.* 'Dialouge', transposed to F
4	Thus the gloomy world at first	*The Fairy Queen.* Song, transposed to B flat
5v	Come, all ye songsters	*The Fairy Queen.* Song, transposed to B flat
6v	May the god of wit inspire	*The Fairy Queen.* Song, arranged from a trio
7v	Hark, how all things with one sound	*The Fairy Queen.* Song.
8v	Thrice happy lovers may you be	*The Fairy Queen.* Song, with slight variants
10v	I looked and saw within the book of fate	*The Indian Emperor.* Song
12	Now the night is chas'd away	*The Fairy Queen.* Song, with slight variants
13	Hark, the echoing air	*The Fairy Queen.* Song, with slight variants in the bass
14	Turn then thine eyes	*The Fairy Queen.* Song, arranged from a duet
15v	No, no, poor suff'ring heart	*Cleomenes, the Spartan Hero.* Song
16v	In vain 'gainst love I strove	*Henry II, King of England.* Song
17v	Yes, Daphne, in your face I find	*The Fairy Queen.* Song. The original has 'Xansi' for 'Daphne' and 'looks' for 'face'
18v	Corinna is divinely fair	Song
19v	Thus to a ripe consenting maid	*The Old Bachelor.* Song.
20v	'Tis Nature's voice	*Hail, bright Cecilia:* Ode for St. Cecilia's Day, 1692. Song, transposed to D
22v	Thou tun'st this world	*Hail, bright Cecilia:* Ode for St. Cecilia's Day, 1692. Song
23v	The fife and all the harmony	*Hail, bright Cecilia:* Ode for St. Cecilia's Day, 1692. Song, transposed to A
25	April who till now	*Celebrate this festival:* Ode for Queen Mary's birthday, 1693. Song
26v	Kindly treat Maria's day	*Celebrate this Festival:* Ode for Queen Mary's birthday, 1693. Song
27v	Ah! cruel nymph, you give despair	Song
29v	Behold the man that with gigantic might	*The Richmond Heiress, or A Woman once in the Right.* 'A Dialouge between a Mad Man & Mad Woman'
34v	I see she flies me	*Aureng-Zebe.* Song
36	I love and I must	'Bell Barr'. Song
37v	Come let us leave the town	*The Fairy Queen.* 'a 2'
39v	Not all my torments can your pity	Song
40v	Fair Chloe my breast so alarms	Duet
43v	What can we poor females do?	Song

Folios	Titles	Sources, and compilers' notes
44v	Celia frowns whene'er I woo her	*The Double Dealer*. Song. The original has 'Cynthia' for 'Celia'
46v	What a sad fate is mine (first setting)	Song. Voice part and a few passages of the bass only
48v	When first I saw the bright Aurelia's eyes	*The Prophetess, or the History of Dioclesian*. Song
50v	Since from my dear	*The Prophetess, or the History of Dioclesian*. Song; the bass lacks all but the last ten bars and two bars to begin the reprise of the second section
51v	Sawney is a bonny lad	Song
52v	Leave these useless arts in loving	*Epsom Wells*. Song, arranged from a duet
53v	I sigh'd and own'd my love	*The Fatal Marriage, or the Innocent Adultery*. Song
55v	There's not a swain on the plain	*Rule a Wife and Have a Wife*. Song
56v	Strike the viol	*Come ye sons of art away*: Ode for Queen Mary's birthday, 1694. Song
57v	Olinda in the shades unseen	Song
58v	I fain would be free	Song. Voice part only (no bass known)
59v	[I burn, I burn]	*The Comical History of Don Quixote*, part ii. The beginning of the words only (no music by Purcell known). A setting by John Eccles of this text appears in *Don Quixote*. Purcell may have intended either only to copy this song (which, as sung by Mrs. Bracegirdle, inspired his own 'Whilst I with grief'—*see* note to f.67v below) or to compose a setting of his own
60v	Ah! how sweet it is to love	*Tyrannic Love, or the Royal Martyr*. Song. Voice part only
61v	Let the dreadful engines	*The Comical History of Don Quixote*, part i. Song. Voice part and a few notes of the bass only
66v	Lucinda is bewitching fair	*Abdelazer, or the Moor's Revenge*. Song. Voice part only
67v	Whilst I with grief	*The Spanish Friar, or the Double Discovery*. Song. Unfinished, with space to continue. 'On Mrs. Bracegirdle Singing (I Burn &c) in the play of Don Quixote.'
69v	Ah! what pains, what racking thoughts	Song. Voice part only (no bass known). Unfinished, with space to continue
70v	'Tis vain to fly like wounded deer	Song. Not Henry Purcell's autograph. Attributed to Daniel Purcell in *Thesaurus Musicus* (London, 1696)

Folios	Titles	Sources, and compilers' notes
72v	What ungrateful devil makes you come?	Song. Not Henry Purcell's autograph; the handwriting is the same as that of the previous song. Attributed to Daniel Purcell in *Gentleman's Journal*, 1693

Reverse end (upside down)

77v	Since, Chloris, the power of your charms	Song. Voice part and first note of the bass only (no complete copy known). This setting is probably not by Purcell. It is not in his hand; the hand is different from that of ff. 70–73

(v) MISCELLANEOUS MANUSCRIPTS

Titles	Sources	Genres and compilers' notes
Behold now, praise the Lord	B.M. Add. MS. 30932, f.121 (the first system of the opening symphony on a pasted-on slip, f.121* (*see* under 'Sonata' below))	Verse anthem with strings
Benedicite (from the *Morning Service* in B flat)	Bodleian MS.Mus.a.1 (the sole item)	Service. For one passage on p. 2 there are two versions. For a note on the reverse side of the second version *see* under Monteverdi in Section II
Blessed are they that fear the Lord	B.M.Add. MS.30931, f.61	Verse anthem with strings
The Fairy Queen	Royal Academy MS.1 (the sole item)	Opera

Only a small part of this score is autograph, as follows:
2a First part of the Second Music, f.3 (partly autograph)
2b Rondeau, f.4
6 First Act Tune, f.20
26 Third Act Tune, f.54v
35 See my many-colour'd fields, f.77 (partly autograph)
38 Fourth Act Tune, f.81v
49 Sure the dull god of marriage, f.97 (partly autograph)
51 Chaconne, f.165v (probably autograph)

Hail, bright Cecilia	Bodleian MS.Mus.c.26, f.22	Ode for St. Cecilia's Day, 1692 Very largely autograph; from half-way through f.67 to the end (f.69v) it is in the hands of two copyists
I was glad	Barber MS.5001, p. 292	Verse Anthem with Strings

Titles	Sources	Genres, and compilers' notes
In the midst of life (first version)	B.M.Add.MS.30931, f.81	Funeral sentences
In thee, O Lord, do I put my trust	Bodleian MS.Mus.c.26, f.10	Verse anthem with strings
Let mine eyes run down with tears	Bodleian MS.Mus.c.26, f.4	Verse anthem
		Second versions of two passages are inserted over the first versions
My beloved spake (first version)	B.M.Add.MS.30932, f.87	Verse anthem with strings
My heart is fixed	Barber MS.5001, p. 308	Verse anthem with strings
O give thanks	Fitzwilliam MS.152 (32 F 23), p. 56	Verse anthem
		An organ score, dated '1693'. The last page (p. 61) is not autograph
Of old when heroes	B.M.MS. Egerton 2596 (the sole item)	Ode (Yorkshire Feast Song)
Out of the deep	B.M.Add.MS.30931, f.67	Verse anthem
Plung'd in the confines of despair	Barber MS.5001, p. 328	Hymn
Sonata for three violins and continuo	B.M.Add.MS.30932, f.121*v	Sonata
		Three lines of the beginning of the second violin part (marked 'flute') already on the reverse side of the slip used for the first system of 'Behold now, praise the Lord' (*see* above), probably in Purcell's hand. In the Purcell Society edition, vol. XIIIa (London, 1921), p. xi, it is printed a third too low[1]
The Lord is my light	Barber MS.5001, p. 276	Verse anthem with strings
Thou knowest, Lord, the secrets of our hearts (first setting, first version)	B.M.Add.MS.30931, f.83	Funeral sentences
Who can from joy refrain?	B.M.Add.MS.30934, f.79	Ode for the Duke of Gloucester's birthday, 1695
Who hath believed our report?	B.M.Add.MS.30932, f.94	Verse anthem

[1] Also cf. G. E. P. Arkwright's query in *Musical Antiquary*, I, 1909-10, p. 128.

II. WORKS NOT BY PURCELL BUT IN HIS HAND[1]

Composers	Titles	Sources	Genres, and compilers' notes
Anon	Holy, holy	Fitzwilliam MS.152 (32 F 23), p. 54	Service. An organ score
Humfrey	By the waters of Babylon	B.M.Add.MS.30932, f.52	Verse anthem. It has been said that Purcell adapted this anthem but this is probably not so.
Monteverdi	Cruda Amarilli	Bodleian MS.Mus.a.1, p.2	Madrigal. For the second version of a short passage in his 'Benedicite' (from the *Morning Service* in B flat) (*see* Section I (v)) Purcell used the blank side of a leaf containing on the other side the beginning of his transcription of this madrigal from Monteverdi's '*Il quinto libro de madrigali*' (Venice, 1605). What remains is a slightly altered version of the first few bars of the top four voices, with the first two words only[2]

III. SUPPOSITITIOUS AUTOGRAPHS

This is a list of manuscripts which have been described in authoritative printed sources as wholly or partly autograph, concerning whose authenticity no refutation appears hitherto to have been published. In our opinion they are certainly not autographs.

Sources	Works
B.M.Add.MS.5337, f.27	The Music in *Bonduca*
B.M.Add.MS.17784	Bass parts of anthems
B.M.Add.MS.33240, f.1	Basso continuo part of 'Welcome to all the pleasures' (Ode for St. Cecilia's Day, 1683)[3]
Bodleian MS.Mus.c.27*	Who can from joy refrain? (Ode for the Duke of Gloucester's birthday, 1695)

[1] The works listed here are those not listed in Section I.

[2] cf. Franklin Zimmerman, 'Purcell and Monteverdi' (*Musical Times*, July 1958, pp. 368-9) and Plate II.

[3] A. Hughes-Hughes, having stated in 'Henry Purcell's Handwriting' (*Musical Times*, 1896, p. 81) that this is not an autograph, labelled it '*Autograph*' in the *Catalogue of Manuscript Music in the British Museum*, II (London, 1908), p. 211.

Sources	Works
Bodleian MS.Mus.c.27, f.3	The songs in *Don Quixote*
Bodleian MS.Mus.c.28, f.78	Now does the glorious day appear (Ode for Queen Mary's birthday, 1689)
Fitzwilliam MS.152 (32 F 23), p. 55	Organ score of Gloria in G (anonymous here, but by O. Gibbons)
Library of Congress, Washington, D.C., MS.ML96.P.89	Song, Underneath this myrtle shade (*The Epicure*)
Sibley	A manuscript containing the *12 Sonatas of III parts* (London, 1683)
Stanford, MS.1	*Te Deum and Jubilate* in D, and song, When first Dorinda's piercing eyes

IV. RELIABLE NON-AUTOGRAPH MANUSCRIPT SOURCES OF MAJOR WORKS BY PURCELL

Works	Sources
Dido and Aeneas[1]	Tenbury MS. 1266
The Fairy Queen	Royal Academy MS.1 (partly autograph—*see* Section I (v))
The Indian Queen	B.M.Add.MSS.31449, 31453, f. 39, and 31455
King Arthur	Royal Academy MS.3
The Prophetess, or the History of Dioclesian	Tenbury MS.1266; B.M.Add.MS.31455
The Tempest, or the Enchanted Island	Tenbury MS.1266
Morning and Evening Service in B flat	Fitzwilliam MS.117 (30 G 10), p. 231rev
Te Deum and Jubilate in D	Stanford, MS.1 (cf. Section III); York Minster Library MS.M.9.s.
12 Sonatas of III parts	Conservatoire Royale de Musique, Brussels, MS.V.14.981 (said to have been copied from the autograph)
	B.M. Royal Music MS.20.h.9, f.98v; a MS. in Sibley (cf. Section III); Gresham College, London, MS.VI.4.19
10 Sonatas of IV parts	Gresham College, London, MS.VI.4.19

[1] *See* Appendix C for recent information about the manuscript of *Dido and Aeneas* in Tokyo. [Editor.]

Appendix B

FURTHER SEVENTEENTH- AND EIGHTEENTH-CENTURY EVIDENCE BEARING ON THE PERFORMANCE OF PURCELL'S WORKS

Compiled by ROBERT DONINGTON

THE quotations printed below make interesting reading for the light they throw on the interpretation of Purcell's music, not as we see it today, but as its own contemporaries and near-contemporaries would have seen it. They contain, in fact, some of the evidence on which the conclusions in Chapter 8 are based. Such evidence is not always available from sources as near in time and place as we could wish, but none of the following is far distant, and taken together we believe it builds up a picture as authentic as it is in some ways unexpected.

GENERAL

[A composer must needs] be transported with some Musical fury; so that himself scarcely knoweth what he doth, nor can presently give a reason of his doing. . . .

Charles Butler, *Principles of Musick* (London, 1636), p. 92.

But when that *Vast-Conchording-Unity* of the whole *Congregational-Chorus* came (as I may say) Thundering in, even so, as it made the very *Ground shake* under us; (Oh the unutterable ravishing Soul's delight!) In the which I was so transported, and *wrapt* up into *High Contemplations*, that there was no room left in my *whole Man*, viz. *Body, Soul* and *Spirit*, for any thing below *Divine* and *Heavenly Raptures*. . . .

Thomas Mace, *Musick's Monument* (London, 1676), p. 19.

ACCIDENTALS

As for the ♭ . . . [except in the key signature] it serves only for that particular Note before which it is placed. . . . [The] ♭ takes away a *Semitone* from the sound of the Note before which it is set, to make it more *grave* or *flat*: [the] ♯ doth add a *Semitone* to the Note to make it more *acute* or sharp: . . . [except in the key-signature] it serves only for that particular Note before which it is applied.

Christopher Simpson, *Compendium* (London, 1665), ed. of 1732, p. 5.

ORNAMENTAL EMBELLISHMENTS

A piece of music can be beautiful, and please not, for want of being performed with the necessary embellishments, of which embellishments the most part are not marked on the paper, whether because in fact they cannot be marked for lack of symbols for the purpose, or whether it has been considered that too many marks encumber and take away the clearness of a melody, and would bring a kind of confusion.

Bénigne de Bacilly, *L'Art de Bien Chanter* (Paris, 1668), p. 135.

[The boy singer Jemmy Bowen] when practising a Song set by *Mr. Purcell*, some of the Music told him to grace and run a Division in such a Place. *O let him alone*, said *Mr. Purcell*; *he will grace it more naturally than you or I can teach him*.[1]

Anthony Aston, *Brief Supplement to Colley Cibber, Esq.* (1748), reported by R. W. Lowe in his ed. of Cibber's *Apology*, II (London, 1889), p. 312.

It is the hardest task that can be to pen the manner of artificial [in the sense of 'made with art'] Gracing an upper part. It hath bin attempted, and in print, but with Woefull Effect . . . the Spirit of that art is Incommunicable by wrighting.

Roger North, B.M. Add. MS. 32533, very early eighteenth century, f.106v.

TEMPO AND RUBATO

There being nothing more difficult in Musick then playing of true time, 'tis therefore necessary to be observ'd by all practitioners, of which there are two sorts, Common time and Triple time, & is distinguish'd by this C this ₵ or this 𝄵 mark, the first is a very slow movement, the next a little faster, and the last a brisk and airry time, & each of them has allways to the length of one Semibrief in a barr, which is to be held in playing as long as you can moderately tell four. . . .

Triple time consists of either three or six Crochets in a barr, and is to be known by this $\frac{3}{2}$, this 𝈎𝐢, this 3 or this $\frac{6}{4}$ marke, to the first there is three Minums in a barr, and is commonly play'd very slow, the second has three Crochets in a barr, and they are to be play'd slow, the third has the same as the former but is play'd faster, the last has six Crochets in a barr & is commonly to brisk tunes as Jiggs and Paspys.

Preface (not actually known to be Purcell's) in his posthumous *Choice Collection for the Harpsichord* (London, 1696).

[1] This quotation is cited by Professor. J. A. Westrup in his *Purcell* (London, 1937), p. 76.

Sometimes a *Tripla* consists of three *Semibreves* to a Measure, each *Semibreve* being shorter than a *Minim* in Common Time.

The more *common Tripla*, is three Minims to a Measure, each *Minim* about the length of a *Crochet* in Common Time.

Christopher Simpson, *Compendium* (London, 1665), pp. 13ff.

Time . . . taken now slowly, now swiftly, and even held in the air, according to the expression of the music, or the sense of the words.

The closes, though written quick, are to be performed much drawn out; as the end of the section or close approaches, the tempo should be increasingly held back.

Girolamo Frescobaldi, *Toccatas* (Rome, 1614), Preface, 1.

Adagio and *Grave* . . . import nothing but a very slow movement: *Presto Largo*, *Poco Largo* or *Largo* by it Self, a middle movement: *Allegro*, and *Vivace*, a very brisk, swift and fast movement.

Henry Purcell, *Sonatas of III parts* (London, 1683), Preface.

Time is a various and undetermined thing . . . [there are] grave, adagio, largo, vivace, allegro, presto, and sometimes prestissimo. The first expresses the slowest Movement, and the rest gradually quicker; but indeed they leave it altogether to Practice to determine the precise Quantity. . . . Movements are swifter in triple than in common time . . . the allegro of one species of triple is a quicker Movement than that of another, so very uncertain these things are.

Alexander Malcolm, *Treatise of Musick* (Edinburgh, 1731), p. 394.

An allegro . . . ought never to exceed a controlled and reasonable movement.

Joachim Quantz, *Essay* (Berlin, 1752), XII, 11.

[In slow movements, avoid] the error of a sluggish, dragging performance.

C. P. E. Bach, *Essay* (Berlin, 1753), transl. W. Mitchell (London, 1949), p. 152.

RHYTHM: DOTTED NOTES, ETC.

It is not possible to determine exactly the time of the little note which follows the dot.

Joachim Quantz, *Essay* (Berlin, 1752), XI, 21.

The short notes which follow dots are always made shorter than the written text indicates.

C. P. E. Bach, *Essay* (Berlin, 1753), p. 113.

Although the values of the Treble do not seem to fit with those of the Bass, it is customary to write thus.

François Couperin, *Pièces de Clavecin*, Bk. II (Paris, 1717), note to 10th Ordre.

PHRASING AND ARTICULATION

On the last note of . . . passages . . . you must pause, even if this note is a quaver or a semiquaver . . . for such a pause avoids confusion between one phrase and another.

Girolamo Frescobaldi, *Toccatas* (Rome, 1614), Preface, 4.

In proper places . . . make a kind of Cessation, or standing still, sometimes Longer, and sometimes Shorter, according to the Nature, or requiring . . . of the Musick.

Thomas Mace, *Musick's Monument* (London, 1676), p. 109.

You must not join notes which should be detached, nor detach notes which should be joined. The notes should not sound as if they were stuck together with glue. On wind instruments the tongue should give articulation, on stringed instruments the bow. . . . Ideas which belong together should not be separated, but when their sense is completed they should be made separate, whether a pause is shown or not.

Joachim Quantz, *Essay* (Berlin, 1752), X, 10.

If by your Manner of Bowing you lay a particular Stress on the Note at the Beginning of every Bar, so as to render it predominant over the rest, you alter and spoil the true Air of the Piece.

Francesco Geminiani, *Art of Playing on the Violin* (London 1740), ed. of 1751, p. 9.

TEXTURE AND DYNAMICS

If in the beginning of the composition an elegant fugal subject occurs, this must be produced with a clearer and more decisive voice . . . and the succeeding voices, if they begin the same fugal subject, . . . are to be enunciated in the same way: this is to be observed in all the voices, when renewed fugal entries occur, so that the coherence and arrangement of all the fugal entries can be heard.

Hermann Finck, *Practica Musica* (Wittenberg, 1556), Lib. V, p. 7.

Entries should be emphasized a little so as to be instantly and clearly perceived by the hearer.

Ludovico Zacconi, *Prattica di Musica* (Rome, 1592), LXVI, p. 59.

Keep still an equal Sound [except in a point of imitation]. . . .

Charles Butler, *Principles of Musick* (London, 1636), p. 98.

Always keep the advantage of being able to produce, at need, after the *forte* a *fortissimo*, and after the *piano* a *pianissimo*. . . . For to perform a whole piece in one uniform manner and with a melody always equal, in short to keep, so to speak, always the same colour: that becomes tedious. Increase or abate the tone as required.

Joachim Quantz, *Essay* (Berlin, 1752), pp. 92 and 108.

Dissonances are generally played more loudly and consonances more softly, because the former stimulate and exacerbate the emotions, while the latter calm them.

C. P. E. Bach, *Essay* (Berlin, 1753), I, 3.

INSTRUMENTAL STYLE AND TEXTURE

A Handsom-Smooth-Sweet-Smart-Clear Stroke; or else Play not at all.

Thomas Mace, *Musick's Monument* (London, 1676), p. 248.

[Vibrato] imitates a certain sweet agitation of the Voice on [instrumental] Sounds; that is why one uses it in all circumstances when the length of the Note allows of it; and it must last as long as the Note.

Jean Rousseau, *Traité de la Viole* (Paris, 1687), p. 100.

Appendix C

A NOTE ON THE NANKI COLLECTION OF PURCELL'S WORKS

IMOGEN HOLST

When the W. H. Cummings library was sold at Sotheby's in 1917, a 'remainder' of over four hundred items was bought by the late Marquis Tokugawa and sent to Tokyo to form part of the Nanki Library. The 'Catalogue of the W. H. Cummings Collection in the Nanki Music Library', published in Tokyo in 1925, mentions the following works by Purcell:

12 Sonatas of III parts, for 2 violins and bass. (3 MSS. and two printed) folio, 5 vols. Playford and Carr, London, 1683.

Ten sonatas in four parts, for 2 violins and bass, bass parts, 1693.

An ode performed upon the Duke of Gloucester's birthday, 1695. (Copies from composer's own MS. by V. Novello and S. Wesley.) obl. 8vo.

Dido and Aeneas, folio, Saec. XVIII.

Indian Queen. (Full score) obl. folio.

Other references to Purcell in the catalogue include:

Purcell, Birds (*sic*) Tallis, &c.
Church Services

Early manuscript scores (containing 21 pieces by 6 composers) folio. Saec. XVIII

Purcell, Blow, Croft and others.
A collection of music compositions (written by different hands) folio.

Purcell, Blow, Tallis, &c.
Anthems.
(containing 29 pieces by 11 composers in full-score with autograph of Dr. Blow.) folio. Saec. XVIII

The *Dido and Aeneas* is the copy which Cummings mentions in the preface to his edition of the opera, published by the Purcell Society in 1889. In this preface he also mentions 'an old set of instrumental and vocal parts which had been used in performance'. These he collated with his own manuscript score and the Ouseley MS. (now Tenbury 1266). Unfortunately he left no record in his Purcell Society edition of where his own manuscript score had differed from the Tenbury MS. or from the set of parts, with the result that since 1917 no other editor has been able to find out what the Cummings MS. contained.

When Edward J. Dent prepared his edition of the work for the Oxford University Press in 1925 he made a fresh collation of the available manuscripts. He was able to see the set of parts, which he refers to as representing the concert version printed by the Musical Antiquarian Society in 1841. But he was not able to see the Cummings score; he was not even aware that it was in Japan.

This started the legend of the 'lost' manuscript of *Dido*. Other legends have grown during the last few years. One of the most recent was the legend that the score was in the possession of an American collector, that it had been locked up in a cellar in Baltimore and that all enquirers were turned away without being allowed to see it. By the beginning of 1958 this particular legend had become alarmingly persistent, so I wrote to Professor Anthony Lewis, to ask if there were any truth in it. He replied: 'It would be an understatement to say that the position is obscure'; and he advised me to write to Dr. J. M. Coopersmith of the Library of Congress in Washington. Dr. Coopersmith wrote that in 1956 he had been asked to expertize a portion of the Nanki Library which had been offered for sale in America, but that, to his regret, he found no Purcell manuscript in the collection.

Meanwhile, Benjamin Britten was revising his edition of the opera for publication, and was trying to make up his mind about several inconsistencies in the Tenbury MS. When I told him of the rumours about the 'lost' Cummings MS. he asked his friend Mr. Reginald Close, who had been British Council representative in Tokyo for many years, if he could get any reliable information about the score. By that time the galley proofs of this book had been corrected and I was beginning to wonder if even the unfailing patience of the Oxford University Press would allow me to take much longer over the search. And then an exciting letter arrived from Miss Seymour Whinyates, Director of the Music Department of the British Council, telling us that Mr. W. R. McAlpine, Deputy Director of the British Council in Tokyo, with the help of Mr. Keiser Sakka and Miss Dorothy Britton, had had an interview with Mr. Kyuhei Oki, the present owner of the *Dido* manuscript, and that Mr. Oki was most generously allowing Mr. Britten to see a microfilm of the score.

The future of the manuscript is still uncertain, but further letters from Tokyo have brought the welcome news that Mr. Oki does not intend to let it go out of his hands unless he is sure that it will be available for research. This statement is in itself a valuable contribution to musicology, and will bring Mr. Oki the gratitude of all lovers of Purcell's music. Mr. Oki has also suggested that it may be possible to arrange a loan exhibition of the manuscript in England during 1959, as part of the celebration of Purcell's tercentenary.

The Oki MS. contains the same amount of music as the Tenbury MS. The missing end of Act II (see p. 25) is not, alas, included. The first nine pages are in a later hand than the rest of the manuscript: they date from the second half of the nineteenth century, and contain editor's marks such as '*sf*, *pp*, *cres*, *Allegretto Grazioso*', &c. In these pages Belinda is Anna, as in the Musical Antiquarian edition of 1841;—she sings an octave lower, in the alto clef. Then, on page 10, the writing changes to early nineteenth century (approximately 1800 to 1810), and remains the same for the rest of the work. Belinda becomes her true self, and all main essentials in the work are the same as in the Tenbury MS.

It seems possible that both the Tenbury MS. and the Oki MS. were copied, at different times and in different hands, from the same earlier manuscript of which no traces have so far been discovered. Several obvious mistakes in copying are identical in the Tenbury and the Oki manuscripts, though on the whole the Oki MS. is the more accurate of the two in ordinary details of copying where there can be no question of any alternative interpretation.

In the Oki MS. time signatures are modernized, 3 becoming $\frac{3}{4}$, &c. Key signatures are modernized: three flats for C minor and four for F minor, compared with Tenbury's two and three. Double bars are added at the end of each short section, contradicting the continuity of the Tenbury MS. Accidentals are sometimes, but not always, modernized. For instance, the second half of the third bar of the Ground in 'Oft she visits' has the written natural and flat that were not considered necessary in the Tenbury MS. Dynamics are not altered: the Oki copyist keeps to Purcell's 'soft' and 'loud'.

Many of the final cadences differ considerably in their melodic interpretation from the written graces of Tenbury. In 'Fear no danger', the end of the line 'The Hero loves as well as you' is given three crotchets in the last bar but one instead of the familiar crotchet and minim. Elsewhere, the cadences in Oki are 'plainer' than in Tenbury:—'this open air' and 'Carthage flames tomorrow' are written as straightforward crotchets.

One of the most illuminating results of comparing the two manuscripts is finding that they agree in several of the 'awkward' passages that editors have fought shy of. Near the end of 'To the hills and the vales', at 'the triumphs of love and of beauty', both manuscripts have a falling augmented fourth in the soprano, involving consecutive sevenths with the bass. Neither Cummings nor Dent found the cadence acceptable: each of them smoothed it out and offered his own alternative.

This is one of many details in the Oki MS. which may bring us nearer to what Purcell intended.[1]

[1] Mr. Britten wishes to acknowledge his gratitude to Mr. Oki for his kindness in allowing these details of information about his manuscript to be given in this book.

INDEX

*Printed in Great Britain by
The Camelot Press Ltd., London and Southampton*